MARIE CURIE

Mother of Modern Physics

Janice Borzendowski

STERLING

New York / London
www.sterlingpublishing.com/kids

To my niece, Jaycee, who I imagined sitting next to me as I was telling Marie's story.

Thanks to my dear friends, Maureen Drexel, Micheline Frederick, Katherine Weissman, and Susan Bierzychudek, for brainstorming with me and keeping me on track. Thanks, also, to my friend and physics/chemistry tutor, Steve Guty, for reviewing the manuscript and for being patient as I struggled to understand what came so easily to Marie Sklodowska-Curie.

STERLING and the distinctive Sterling logo are registered trademarks of Sterling Publishing Co., Inc.

Library of Congress Cataloging-in-Publication Data
Borzendowski, Janice.
  Marie Curie : mother of modern physics / Janice Borzendowski.
    p. cm. — (Sterling biographies)
  Includes bibliographical references and index.
  ISBN 978-1-4027-5318-3 (pbk.) — ISBN 978-1-4027-6543-8 (hardcover)
  1. Curie, Marie, 1867-1934—Juvenile literature. 2. Physicists—Poland—Biography—Juvenile literature. 3. Women physicists—Poland—Biography—Juvenile literature. 4. Physicists—France—Biography—Juvenile literature. 5. Women physicists—France—Biography—Juvenile literature. 6. Chemists—Poland—Biography—Juvenile literature. 7. Women chemists—Poland—Biography—Juvenile literature. 8. Chemists—France—Biography—Juvenile literature. 9. Women chemists—France—Biography—Juvenile literature. I. Title.
  QD22.C8B67 2009
  540.92—dc22
  [B]

2008030701

10 9 8 7 6 5 4 3 . 2 1

Published by Sterling Publishing Co., Inc.
387 Park Avenue South, New York, NY 10016
© 2009 by Janice Borzendowski

Distributed in Canada by Sterling Publishing
c/o Canadian Manda Group, 165 Dufferin Street
Toronto, Ontario, Canada M6K 3H6
Distributed in the United Kingdom by GMC Distribution Services
Castle Place, 166 High Street, Lewes, East Sussex, England BN7 1XU
Distributed in Australia by Capricorn Link (Australia) Pty. Ltd.
P.O. Box 704, Windsor, NSW 2756, Australia

Printed in China
All rights reserved

Sterling ISBN 978-1-4027-5318-3 (paperback)
          ISBN 978-1-4027-6543-8 (hardcover)

Image research by Larry Schwartz

For information about custom editions, special sales, premium and corporate purchases, please contact Sterling Special Sales Department at 800-805-5489 or specialsales@sterlingpublishing.com.

Contents

Events in the Life of Marie Curie

1867

November 7, 1867
Maria Salomea Sklodowska is born in Warsaw, Poland, to Bronislava Boguska Sklodowska and Wladislaw Sklodowski.

May 8, 1878
Maria's mother dies of tuberculosis.

June 12, 1883
Maria graduates first in her class from a Russian-run high school.

January 1886
Maria begins working as a governess. Has a failed romance.

November 1891
Marie moves to Paris to begin her studies at the Sorbonne.

July 1893
Marie graduates first in her class in physics.

1894
In spring, Marie meets Pierre Curie. In July, she graduates second in her class in mathematics.

July 26, 1895
Marie Sklodowska marries Pierre Curie.

August 1896
Marie becomes certified as a physics teacher.

September 12, 1897
Marie gives birth to Irène. Later that year, decides to pursue her PhD in physics.

1898
On July 18, the Curies announce the discovery of polonium, named for Marie's homeland; on December 26, they announce the discovery of radium.

June 25, 1903
Marie becomes the first woman to earn a PhD from the Sorbonne.

December 10, 1903
The Curies, with Henri Becquerel, are awarded the Nobel Prize in Physics.

December 6, 1904
The Curies' second daughter, Ève, is born.

April 19, 1906
Pierre is run over by a horse-drawn wagon and is killed instantly. Marie is appointed to his position as physics professor at the Sorbonne.

1909
The Sorbonne agrees to build the Radium Institute.

February 25, 1910
Dr. Eugène Curie, Pierre's father, dies. In November, Marie presents herself as a candidate to the French Academy of Sciences but is rejected.

November 4, 1911
Marie is accused of having an affair with a married man, Paul Langevin. About a month later, she learns she has been awarded her second Nobel Prize—this time in chemistry.

1914–1918
Shortly after Marie is appointed director of the physics and chemistry lab at the Radium Institute in 1914, she puts her work on hold during World War I to take X-ray equipment to the battlefield and train others to use the equipment.

1921
Marie and her daughters travel to the United States to receive a gram of radium from President Warren Harding.

1930
Marie undergoes the last of four surgeries to remove her cataracts; continues to work at the Radium Institute.

1933
Marie suffers a gall bladder attack; refuses an operation.

July 4, 1934
Following a bout with the flu, Marie Curie dies in eastern France. She is buried in Sceaux, her coffin placed on top of Pierre's. In 1995, both their coffins are moved to the Pantheon in Paris.

1934

A Glow in the Dark

The glowing tubes looked like faint, fairy lights.

Paris, the "City of Lights," was dark in the neighborhood of Boulevard Kellermann. The little two-story house at 108 was mostly dark, too. Downstairs, Marie Sklodowska-Curie sat down to take up her sewing, while her husband Pierre paced around the room. Though quiet, they both seemed restless, distracted.

It was no good pretending—they both knew where they wanted to be, even though they had left the place only a few hours earlier. As if in silent agreement, they put on their coats and went out onto the street, two shadowy figures walking as one to their laboratory.

Few but these two would go so far as to call this structure a laboratory, for it was really just a run-down, wooden shed. Yet it was here that Marie and Pierre Curie had discovered two new chemical elements—polonium and radium—the latter destined to change not just the course of science but also the course of the world.

As the two opened the door to their work space that night, they did not need lanterns to find their way. The blue-green glow of radium led the way, as it was about to light the way into their future.

CHAPTER 1

Youngest and Brightest

I was only six years old, and because I was the youngest and smallest in the class, was frequently brought forward to recite.

On November 7, 1867, Bronislava Boguska Sklodowska and Wladislaw Sklodowski welcomed the last of their five children into the world. Named Maria Salomea Sklodowska, this youngest of her three sisters (Zofie, Bronislava, and Helena) and one brother (Jòzef) would very early show signs that in a family of great minds, hers was exceptional. Although born last in her family, for the rest of her life, Maria, nicknamed Manya, would seldom be anything but first in all she attempted.

Home Schooling

At the time of her birth, the Sklodowski family was living at 16 Freta Street in Warsaw's old city, in a small apartment attached to the private school for girls where her mother was the

Bronislava Boguska Sklodowska, Manya's mother, was a beautiful, well-educated woman. Her early death plunged Manya into depression.

Polish Names

In Poland, a person's last name indicates his or her gender. The most common feminine ending is an *a*; the most common masculine ending is an *i*. Thus, Maria, her mother, and her sisters used *Sklodowska*; her father and brother used *Sklodowski*. The family as a whole was referred to in the masculine—"the Sklodowski family" or "the Sklodowskis."

Like most Polish children, the Sklodowskis all had nicknames. From left: Zofie ("Zosia"), Helena ("Hèla"), Maria ("Manya," as well as many others), Jòzef ("Jozio"), and Bronislava ("Bronya").

Nicknames, too, are very popular in Polish culture. Most Poles from early childhood are called by one or more shortened, or "adapted," versions of their given names. Maria had many nicknames, but most often she was called Manya. Her sister Zofia was called Zosia; Bronislava became Bronya; Helena, Hèla; and Jòzef, Jozio.

This nineteenth-century painting shows Freta Street in Warsaw. The building where Manya was born, number 16, today houses the Marie Sklodowska-Curie Museum.

principal—and had once been a pupil. Her father was also a teacher, of physics and mathematics, at a school for boys. This apartment was not to be her home for long, however. Before she turned one year old, Manya's father accepted a new position as a physics teacher and assistant director at a boy's high school in the western part of the city, and the family moved to living quarters belonging to that institution. At this time, Manya's mother gave up her job, for their new lodgings were much too far for her to travel to work each day.

It was in this new apartment that Manya would spend the early years of her life, in an atmosphere of love and learning. As teachers, her parents incorporated lessons into virtually every one of their children's activities and games. By the time she was four, Manya had already learned to read—without even trying, it seemed. Bored with her own lessons, her older sister Bronya amused herself by playing teacher to her baby sister; and before long, and without anyone realizing it, Manya could read better than Bronya.

Manya was also extremely shy and highly emotional, and it was these two aspects of her character that would be most challenging for her throughout her life. Unlike reading, science, mathematics, and languages, all of which came easily to her, she would have a much more difficult time learning to cope with personal challenges. Sadly, she would be faced with them at a very young age.

As a young girl, Manya liked nothing better than to wander around her father's study while in the background her parents talked of serious matters she could not yet understand. She would pass by all the things she loved in the room one by one—the armchairs covered with rich, red velvet, the green malachite clock, and the precision **barometer** encased in oak. Her favorite was the glass case that contained instruments she found endlessly fascinating—glass tubes, scales, mineral specimens, and an **electroscope**. Her father had told her these were "physics apparatus." Although she did not know what that meant, she liked the sound of those words and repeated them over and over.

This is an electroscope, one of the instruments that fascinated Manya as a child. As an adult, she would use it in her scientific experiments.

Dark Clouds

It cannot be known exactly when Manya first became aware that one of the serious matters her parents were discussing was her mother's health. Bronislava Sklodowska was seriously ill with tuberculosis, a highly contagious lung disease, incurable at the time. As sensitive as Manya was, no doubt she wondered why her mother, whom she adored and admired greatly, always kept her at arm's length. Then there were the long absences, when her

This poster depicts the highly contagious nature of tuberculosis. Manya's mother had to withhold physical affection from her children to avoid passing on the disease to them.

TUBERCULOSIS

DON'T KISS ME!

YOUR KISS OF AFFECTION THE GERM OF INFECTION

TOWN OF HEMPSTEAD, W.H.RUNCIE MD. HEALTH OFFICER
WPA FEDERAL ART PROJECT DISTRICT 4

mother, accompanied by her sister Zosia, traveled far away to healthier climates in an attempt to cure, or at least slow, the progression of the disease.

At the same time her mother was fighting to regain her health, Manya's father was losing the battle with another kind of enemy—one all Poles were fighting: political tyranny. This enemy would have a far-reaching and devastating impact on the family's livelihood for years to come.

Long before Manya's birth, Poland had been taken over by the Russian Empire—with its citizens considered subjects of Tsar Alexander II. So total was this takeover that Poland, a once powerful country, no longer existed officially; it was not even included on maps of the world.

To the Sklodowski family, the Russian Empire had a very personal face. It belonged to her father's supervisor, Principal M. Ivanov, who was loyal to the tsar. He had the power to make or break those who served under him, and he chose to break Wladislaw Sklodowski, who could never successfully hide the fact that he was a proud Polish patriot. In 1873, when the family returned from their summer holidays, they learned that Ivanov had demoted Mr. Sklodowski. Overnight, the family's income was

Tsar Alexander II, ruler of the Russian Empire, considered Polish citizens his subjects. When he was assassinated in 1881, Manya and her best friend were caught by their teacher dancing with joy.

cut dramatically and their home taken away from them.

This forced the Sklodowskis to move several times before settling into an apartment that, for added income, they turned into a boarding house for pupils of Mr. Sklodowski. In 1876, one of those boys carried more than just his belongings into the cramped, noisy quarters. He brought with him the germs of typhus, another highly contagious disease of the day, transmitted by fleas, lice, or mites. Both Zosia and Bronya became infected, and Zosia, age fourteen, did not survive. Manya was eight at the time.

Maria's First School

Grieving the death of her eldest daughter caused Mrs. Sklodowska's condition to worsen, and she realized she did not have long to live. She became more determined than ever to ensure that her two younger daughters would have the best chance for a good education. So, at ten, Manya was enrolled at a private school for girls run by Madame Jadwiga Sikorska. It was clear to one and all that she was a gifted child, and Manya was given advanced placement in a class with older girls, including her sister Hèla.

It was the beginning of what would be a stellar academic career. At the same time, it would mark the beginning of Manya's

Takeover of Poland

Poland, once one of the most powerful kingdoms in the world, had weakened politically over time, leaving it prey to stronger nations. Between 1764 and 1795, Russia, Austria, and Prussia (a former kingdom of north-central Europe) divided Poland's vast lands like pieces of a pie. Russia took the choicest pieces—Warsaw and lands to the east. The goal of the Russian authorities was to erase every trace of Polish culture and its thousands of years of history. They forbade Poles to speak their native language and banned Polish books and periodicals; they even attempted to destroy the Poles' religious faith.

Twice the Poles took up arms against their Russian captors, first in November 1830 and again in January 1863. Both uprisings proved disastrous for the Poles, resulting in death, exile, and imprisonment for thousands and the loss of property for countless others.

This map shows how Poland was divided by Russia, Austria, and Prussia.

firsthand experience of life under the rule of the Russian dictators. As Manya was soon to realize, the Polish people had lost their military and political power, but their spirits remained strong, and they were determined to keep their language, customs, and traditions alive. When armed resistance failed, they turned to secret tactics that centered on education. The new heroes would be the intellectuals—artists, scientists, and schoolteachers.

Among those new heroes were Madame Sikorska and the teachers in her school, who faced danger every day by teaching their students both the official Russian curriculum and, in secret, Polish culture. Teaching the forbidden subjects put everyone in danger and under constant pressure, yet no one questioned the importance of taking the risk. The students

. . . Manya was given advanced placement in a class with older girls, including her sister, Hèla.

and teachers at Manya's school never knew when they might receive a surprise visit from one of the Russian inspectors, whose job it was to make sure that the Poles were following the rules.

All the girls at Madame Sikorska's knew to be alert to the sound of a signal-bell—two long rings followed by two short rings. That was the sign to quickly scoop up all remnants of Polish schoolwork, hide them, and be back in their chairs, sitting calmly and pretending to be hard at work on the approved Russian material, by the time the inspector walked in. Sometimes there was less than a moment's notice before he would burst into the classroom and demand a demonstration of one student's knowledge. Inevitably, it was the youngest and brightest in the class the teacher called on. Manya, though fighting back tears and the urge to run, never failed to answer every one of the inspector's questions perfectly—and in flawless Russian.

Everyone was relieved when the inspector left, well satisfied. Manya, however, was slow to recover from these ordeals.

Difficult Transitions and First Success

Fewer than three years after her sister Zosia died, Manya's mother lost her battle with tuberculosis in 1878; she was only forty-two years old. Her death was devastating to ten-year-old Manya. She would later write, "This catastrophe was the first great sorrow of my life and threw me into a profound depression."

The remaining Sklodowskis grew even closer, but Manya's father was a changed man, worn down by grief, professional defeat, and near financial ruin due to bad investments. Still, he remained dedicated to the education of his children.

When Manya was fourteen, Mr. Sklodowski took her out of the comforting atmosphere of Madame Sikorska's in favor of a government-run high school, called a *gymnasium*. It is not known why he chose to place her in this unfamiliar and unwelcoming environment—the Russian teachers were known to treat the Polish students harshly and unfairly. He probably felt it would improve her educational and career chances later, because only government-run institutions could award graduation

Mr. Sklodowski, seated here with his three daughters (left to right: Manya, Bronya, and Hèla), always supported higher education for women.

certificates; plus, her older sister Bronya and brother Jozio had graduated from the same school.

It could not have been easy to adjust to her new environment, but Manya's powerful desire to learn and her strict self-discipline were enough to ensure her academic success. She also soon formed a close friendship with a classmate, Kazia Przyboroska, the daughter of a librarian. Walking together each day to school, they played typical childish games, and they were fiercely united in their patriotic spirit. They made sure, every day, to spit on a statue erected to those Poles who were loyal to the Russian tsar. Then, on the day they learned Tsar Alexander II had been killed by an assassin, they were caught by the school superintendent dancing in the street.

Over time, Manya even came to enjoy the school, despite the hated Russian administrators and teachers. On June 12, 1883, following in the footsteps of her sister and brother, she became the third member of the family to receive the gold medal awarded to the number-one graduate in her class. As she walked home that day with her proud father, she

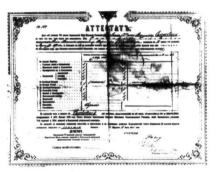

Shown here is Manya Sklodowska's high school diploma. She graduated at the top of her class, the first of her many firsts.

had in her hand the first of her many firsts—though it would be some time before she would achieve the next one.

A Summer in the Country

Following her graduation from high school, Manya finally was given the time she needed to fully recover from the deaths of her mother and sister and the years of intense study. Her graduation present was a year in the country, a period she would look back on as the only carefree time of her life.

Both sides of Manya's family had ancestors who were landowners, with manor houses and country estates. Though some had lost their properties when Poland lost its independence, many still lived in the countryside, giving the Sklodowski family ready-made vacation spots throughout their lives. Now these homes would offer welcome relief to the worn and grieving Manya.

She went south first to Zwola, where she stayed, alternately, with the families of two of her uncles on her mother's side. She wrote to her best friend Kazia, "Ah, how gay life is at Zwola! There are always a great many people, and a freedom, equality, and independence such as you can hardly imagine." From there it was on to Zawieprzyce and the estate of Uncle Xavier, where free-roaming thoroughbred horses dotted the landscape, on whose backs she would learn to be a horsewoman.

As she walked home that day with her proud father, she had in her hand the first of her many firsts . . .

The winter of her year of leisure, 1883–1884, found her in Skalbmierz, at the home of Uncle Zdzislav and his wife and three daughters. In this noisy, active home set at the foot of the Carpathian Mountains, Manya was swept into a whirlwind of activities whose only purpose was fun and laughter.

The timid and serious Manya seemed to disappear in these months. She threw herself into every activity, giving way to the simple pleasures of being a young girl—flirting with boys and worrying what she should wear to the next party and how to fix her hair.

By July when she returned home to Warsaw, she was a changed girl—she had gained weight, had renewed energy, and was in much better spirits. And the best was yet to come. Upon her return to the city, a former student of her mother's invited Manya and Hèla to spend the rest of the summer at her estate northeast of Warsaw. It was a glorious last fling spent in a beautiful home set in the grassy meadows between two rivers.

In September, the girls' carefree vacation came to an end. They returned to the grimy, hot city, and to yet another new apartment, this one still smaller than the last and in less attractive surroundings. Their new home did, however, offer one major advantage: peace and quiet—there would be no more boarders in the Sklodowski household.

Manya now turned to face her future.

This studio portrait shows Manya Sklodowska in 1883 at age 16.

CHAPTER 2

An Independent Life

Thus, when scarcely eighteen, I left my father's house to begin an independent life.

Following her graduation from high school, Manya had her heart set on an advanced education, but girls were prohibited from going to college in Poland, and she had no money to leave the country to study elsewhere. So for the time being, her path was set: She would work as a private tutor, a governess, and continue her studies at what came to be called the Flying University, an unofficial—and illegal—school system organized by Polish intellectuals.

The Flying University was only a temporary solution, however. If Manya was ever going to make something of herself, she would have to find a way to earn enough money to continue her formal education outside of Poland. Fortunately, her older sister Bronya shared the same dream, and they decided to join forces to make it come true.

The sisters made a pact: Because Bronya was older, she would be given the opportunity first to continue her education. She would begin her medical studies in Paris while Manya stayed behind in Poland to work as a governess for a wealthy family, saving most of her income to help their father pay for Bronya's tuition at the medical school. So January 1886 found Manya Sklodowska on her way to a small manor house in Szczuki, a village some 100 kilometers north of Warsaw. "That going away remains one of the most vivid memories of my youth," she would later

The Flying University

Also known as the Floating University, the Flying University earned its nickname because it had no campus or buildings. To avoid detection by the Russian authorities, classes were held in constantly changing locations. This underground organization was originally formed to give Polish girls the opportunity to continue their educations after high school, but it became so successful that, over time, boys, too, took advantage of the classes taught by Polish scientists, philosophers, historians, and other scholars.

write. "My heart was heavy as I climbed into the railway car. It was to carry me for several hours, away from those I loved."

Living Among Strangers

Fortunately, Manya found her employer, Mr. Zorawski, and his wife and children to be "excellent people." Of the Zorawskis' seven children, Manya had been hired to teach the two elder daughters, Bronka, eighteen, and Andzia, ten. (Three older sons were away at school, and the youngest son and daughter were three years old and six months old, respectively.) It must have been awkward at first for her to teach Bronka, who was so close in age to her, but the two quickly became more like friends than student and teacher.

It did not take Manya long to establish a routine for accomplishing her official duties; and though she worked long hours most days, she found time to undertake two additional projects that were important to her. The first was in keeping with

Manya worked as a governess from 1886 to 1889 in the Zorawski's home in Szczuki.

the philosophy that had become popular among the Polish intellectual class, called positivism.

Followers of positivism—Manya and her family and friends among them—believed that Poland's best chance to regain its independence was through building a solid educational and scientific foundation among its people. To do that, the positivists believed, they had to take it upon themselves to educate all people, including women and members of the peasant class—typically farmers and their families who were poor and uneducated.

In the manor house in Szczuki, Manya was living literally next door to members of that class. Mr. Zorawski was an estate manager in charge of a beet-sugar factory on the property, and most of the children of the laborers who worked for him were illiterate or knew only Russian—the sole language taught in the village school. She asked the Zorawskis for permission to teach those children to read and write in Polish. Doing so was strictly

Auguste Comte (1798–1857), French mathematician and philosopher, had a philosophy of positivism which was adopted by Polish intellectuals as the way to regain the independence of their country.

forbidden by the government and would put them in danger of imprisonment or deportation to Siberia; nevertheless, the Zorawskis allowed Manya to set up her class. Mrs. Zorawska even allowed her to use her bedroom as a schoolroom and for Bronka to act as her assistant. This increased Manya's respect for the family greatly.

On the surface, the little school was a success: Within a year, attendance grew from ten to eighteen students and sometimes included parents of the children. However, Manya worried whether she could make a lasting difference in these children's lives—they needed more educational help than she could provide on her own.

Manya probably also wished she had more help to carry out her second task: continuing her own studies. She hoped that by reading in a wide range of subjects—science, sociology, literature, mathematics—she would discover what she wanted to focus on when her turn came to become a student at the University of Paris, the world-famous Sorbonne. "I was as much interested in literature and sociology as in science," she would later write.

> . . . she would discover what she wanted to focus on when her turn came to become a student . . .

"However, during these years of isolated work, trying little by little to find my real preferences, I finally turned toward mathematics and physics."

Between her salaried duties and her volunteer teaching of the village children, Manya had little time to continue her studies. Often she could not begin to take up her books and papers until nine o'clock at night; just as often she woke as early as six in the morning to get in a few more hours of study. Still, she pressed on; and at the very least, she later wrote, she "acquired the habit of independent work, and learned a few things which were to be of use later on."

Heartbreak

It was not all work and no play for Manya during this period. She took great pleasure in the beauty of the countryside. Years later, she would remember "the marvelous snow house we made one winter . . . ; we could sit in it and look out across the rose-tinted snow plains."

Nothing, however, would distract her from her work and her future plans more than the appearance of the Zorawskis' eldest son, Casimir, who had come home for the holidays from his studies at Warsaw University. Not even the hardworking, studious Manya could help but be drawn to this nineteen-year-old, handsome, accomplished young man. He, in turn, was swept away by Manya, who was by now growing gracefully into her beauty and was smart, talented, and charming. Soon, the two were in love and talking of marriage.

The future of science—indeed, the future of the world— would have turned out very differently had this wedding taken place. It was not to be, however. The Zorawskis refused to give the couple their blessing. How was this possible? By now, all the members of the family had great affection and respect for Manya. They knew her family; they knew that her ancestors were of the same class as theirs—landowners and aristocrats. Yet all that mattered to them was that, currently, she had no money and no social position. As a governess, a member of the "working class," she was simply not considered good enough to become the wife of their son and heir.

What of Casimir? Did he stand by the woman he loved? In that era, parental approval for two young people to marry was very important—especially for the man or woman who came from

Casimir Zorawski was Manya's first love. Had he been able to stand up to his parents, the future of science would have been very different, indeed.

the "upper class"—and Casimir was unwilling, or did not have the courage, to go against them. Manya was rejected, not just by the man she loved but also by the family she believed had grown to love her as well. It was a double blow.

Overnight everything changed, though on the surface everything remained the same. Remarkably, Manya chose to stay at the Zorawskis, for she was determined to make good on her end of the agreement with Bronya. She could not afford to give up this well-paying job. Perhaps, too, she hoped Casimir and his parents might have a change of heart—she could not give up on love so easily. So, for the time being, she carried out her duties as before.

In Manya's letters home, though, her despair—and sometimes anger—was evident, especially after her sister Hèla's engagement was broken for a similar reason. In May of 1887, she wasted no words in telling her brother Jozio what she thought of such young men: "If they don't want to marry poor young girls, let them go to the devil!" Fortunately, the end of this difficult period was in sight. She lasted another fifteen months with the Zorawskis, during which time she focused on her self-study program. It was a letter from Bronya in 1888 and a change in her father's circumstances that, together, finally made it possible for Manya to return to Warsaw. Her sister had passed her examinations with flying colors and was already working. She was also luckier in love than her two sisters. She and Casimir Dluski, a fellow Pole and medical student, were preparing to be married. Then in April of that year, Manya's father accepted an unpleasant, but well-paying, job as the director of a boy's reform school and could now afford to help Bronya more and to set up a savings account for Manya. Two months later, in June 1889, Manya said good-bye to Szczuki and the Zorawskis.

Eye on the Future

Paris, however, was still out of reach financially, so upon her return to Warsaw, Manya accepted another governess position with the generous and gracious family of an industrialist, the Fuchs. Before she had spent a year with them, she received another letter from Bronya, telling her to come to Paris the next year and live with her and her new husband. Surprisingly, Manya did not respond with joy and excitement but with confusion and uncertainty. She responded to Bronya, "I dreamed of Paris . . . [but] now that the possibility is offered me, I do not know what to do."

Bronya and Mr. Sklodowski joined forces to encourage Manya to keep her sights set on Paris. At last she agreed, but on the condition that she spend another year in Warsaw teaching to earn her travel expenses.

During this year, she again took classes offered by the Flying University, and it was this experience that renewed her

Manya and her older sister and best friend Bronya (sitting) made a pact to help each other earn their way to Paris to get a higher education.

enthusiasm and refueled her drive to make something of her life. In particular, she was thrilled to have, for the first time, the chance to work in a laboratory to conduct experiments. This door was opened to her by her cousin, Joseph Boguski, who ran what was called the Museum of Industry and Agriculture, which was, in fact, a cover for a laboratory used to train Polish scientists.

Sundays and evenings found Manya at the "museum," sometimes taking chemistry courses from her cousin or his colleagues but, more often, working on her own. In describing her attempts to duplicate experiments she read about in chemistry and physics papers, she wrote, "At times I would be encouraged by a little unhoped-for success, at others I would be in the deepest despair because of accidents and failures resulting from my inexperience. But on the whole . . . this first trial confirmed in me the taste for experimental research in the fields of physics and chemistry."

In particular, she was thrilled to have, for the first time, the chance to work in a laboratory to conduct experiments.

Yet she had mixed feelings about leaving Poland. She felt an obligation to stay with her father—and truth be told, she still hoped that things might work out between her and Casimir Zorawski. In September 1891, she met with him one last time. He repeated his fears and excuses, and Manya found she could not bear listening to them anymore. "If you can't see a way to clear up our situation," she told him, "it is not for me to teach it to you."

Eight years had passed since she walked out of high school with her first-place gold medal, and six since she began working as a governess. She was almost twenty-four. It was now or never to make her move.

CHAPTER 3

Paris, and Pierre

[A]t the age of twenty-four . . . I was able to realize the dream that had been always present in my mind for several years.

The changes in Manya Sklodowska's life began almost immediately upon her arrival in the French capital in November 1891, starting with the simple act of filling out her registration form for the first quarter at the Faculty of Science at the Sorbonne. It was at that moment that she signed the French version of her name—Marie, the name by which she would come to be known around the world—for the first time.

To the Dluskis—her sister Bronya and her brother-in-law, Casimir—she remained Manya. Life with them in general felt little different from life in Warsaw, living as they were among a community of other Polish exiles. Soon, however, Marie began to think it was too familiar, too comfortable; and she knew it was much too distracting. Her brother-in-law loved company, and often their household was a center of activity. Too many nights, Marie's concentration on her studies was

This portrait of Marie was taken a few months after her arrival in Paris.

broken by loud music and conversation and calls for her to join the fun. She also could not afford the time or the bus fare for the hour-long commute from the Dluskis' home outside Paris to the university.

Starting from Behind

Within months, the situation began to weigh heavily on Marie, for as she had feared before leaving Poland, her self-study program of the last eight years was no match for the education of her French classmates. At the same time, she faced an unexpected obstacle: the French language. Believing herself to be fluent in French before she arrived, she soon found that when it was spoken rapidly by French natives it was difficult to understand.

So, comforting as it was with the Dluskis, Marie knew she would have to strike out on her own, to put herself into the thick of the academic world in the Latin Quarter—a popular Parisian neighborhood for students and artists—located close to the university, the library, and the laboratories. In March 1892, she found the first of many cheap rooms she would call home during her years as a student. Most mornings there, she would

This photograph shows a modern-day view of the Latin Quarter in Paris, the neighborhood where Marie lived during her student days at the Sorbonne.

wake shivering even under the mountain of clothing she had piled on top of her bedcovers the night before. Her little stove was no match for the cold in her little apartment; besides, she could rarely afford to feed it coal on a regular basis. Often, she had little to eat beyond some bread and a cup of hot chocolate.

But her dreary living conditions were of little concern to her. "My situation was not exceptional," she would later write; "it was the familiar experience of many of the Polish students whom I knew." Besides, outside was Paris! To Marie, all life there seemed a miracle, where no language was forbidden to speak, no newspaper or book forbidden to read. Most importantly, she was, at last, living her dream, free from duties as a governess and free from restrictions on what she could study. She also had the good fortune to be taught by some of the great scientific minds of the day, including her physics professor, Gabriel Lippmann, who in 1908 would win a Nobel Prize for his invention

Gabriel Lippmann, Marie's physics professor, won a Nobel Prize in 1908 for his invention of color photo reproduction.

of color photo reproduction, and her math teacher, Henri Poincaré, who was considered the most brilliant mathematician of the nineteenth century.

Finishing First

The work habits she had established, coupled with her ability to concentrate intensely and for long hours at a stretch, now served her well as she divided her time between her classes, her experimental work in the laboratories, and study in the library. After the library closed at night, she went home to work more, often late into the night, rising early each morning to begin the cycle again.

The days ticked by, one after another, her study routine rarely varying, until final-exam day came in July 1893. Still she felt unprepared. Worse, though, were the long days after the exam, waiting to learn the results—which were to be announced publicly in the auditorium. When the day finally arrived, she found a spot among the crowd of her classmates. Quiet fell over the hall as they awaited the reading of the names of those who had passed and would receive a degree in physics.

> *. . . she divided her time between her classes, her experimental work in the laboratories, and study in the library.*

The names were called out in order of merit. First in the class was the quiet foreigner, and one of only two women in the class: Marie Sklodowska.

Home to Celebrate and Plan Ahead

Now her vacation could begin. She cleaned out her room, stored her meager furnishings at a fellow student's place, and prepared for the journey back to Poland, where she would have three months to rest, relax, and bask in the care of her extended family. She would also use these months to try to find a way to make her dwindling savings stretch another year in Paris, for she was not satisfied with her degree in physics; she also wanted an advanced degree—a master's—in mathematics.

As the weeks went by and the date of her return to Paris drew closer, Marie's financial prospects remained thin. The only thing that had gained weight was Marie herself. Appalled by her loss of weight, wherever she went after her return home at the beginning of the summer, family and friends insisted she eat and eat.

First in the class was the quiet foreigner, and one of only two women in the class: Marie Sklodowska.

With few days left of her summer, she began to lose heart. What she did not know was that behind the scenes a friend and fellow student at the Sorbonne, Jadwiga Dydynska, had recommended Marie for an Alexandrovitch Scholarship, awarded to Polish students studying abroad.

Overnight she had six hundred **rubles**, more than enough to pay her tuition and fees for fifteen months, with money left over to afford a better room on a decent street.

Within the year, and again keeping to her strict schedule of study, Marie had her master's degree in mathematics. Her only disappointment was that she did not graduate first in her class; she had managed only second place this time.

Magnetic Attraction

In the spring of 1894, even before she had completed her mathematics course work, Marie had her first job, thanks to one of her professors at the Sorbonne, Gabriel Lippmann. She had been commissioned by the Society for the Encouragement of National Industry to do a study on the magnetic properties of various steels. The trouble was, the society did not have sufficient

Women's Rights

Marie Sklodowska's accomplishments at the Sorbonne are all the more remarkable when viewed in the context of the times. During the years she was a student there, women in France could not vote, they could not testify in court, and married women could not even spend any money they made without the permission of their husbands. Women were not supposed to live alone, eat in restaurants alone, or go out alone at night. And although French women were permitted to pursue a secondary education, few did so because they did not receive the same elementary education as boys, and so had little chance of passing university-level entrance exams. Ironically, foreign women in France, like Marie, had a better chance of being accepted at universities in the country.

When Marie enrolled at the Sorbonne in 1891, of the total student population of 9,000, only 210 were women. She was one of only two women in the science program when she graduated first in her class in 1893 and one of five when she graduated second in mathematics in 1894.

When Marie Sklodowska enrolled at the world-famous Sorbonne in Paris, there were very few women in attendance.

laboratory space in which she could conduct her experiments, so she set about trying to find it herself.

She mentioned her problem to a friend from her governess days, Professor Joseph Kowalski, who was on his honeymoon in Paris at the time. He told her of a scientist he admired—an expert in **magnetism**—who was working at the Municipal School of Industrial Physics and Chemistry and who might be able to provide her with a place to work. Pierre Curie, he told her, was well-known for going out of his way to help others. Professor Kowalski invited them both to tea so he could introduce them.

Marie first saw the "tall young man with auburn hair and large, limpid eyes," as she would later describe him, standing in the opening of a French window in the apartment of Professor Kowalski. The two hit it off, and Pierre asked to see her again so they could talk more about the scientific and social subjects in which they were both interested and on which they seemed to share similar opinions.

Pierre Curie, born in Paris on May 15, 1859, had much in common with the bright, young Polish graduate student. Both came from close-knit families of highly educated intellectuals with strong patriotic feelings. His grandfather and father were both doctors; his father, Eugène, was honored for his bravery in treating wounded rebels during the French Revolution of 1848 and the Franco-German War of 1870–1871.

Like Marie, Pierre had taken an early interest in literature and poetry but later realized that his future, too, lay in science. Also, as Marie had done, Pierre postponed his graduate studies in order to work to help supplement the family income. Pierre, too, was highly sensitive, with a tendency to suffer from depression and self-doubt. Both were free thinkers, nature lovers, and true patriots; neither was religious.

In 1894, Marie met Pierre Curie, shown in this undated photograph, and found that they shared common interests.

One major difference between them was in their approach to education and scholarly endeavors. Marie was ambitious and always strove to be at the top of her class. Pierre, in contrast, was known to shy away from competition in any form. Although smart, he seemed to have learning disabilities that made it difficult for him to focus in a classroom setting, and so he was schooled at home until he was sixteen. He flourished under private tutoring, enabling him to earn his degree in physics, after which he enrolled in the Sorbonne.

Pierre Curie's Scientific Work

Pierre Curie's first job following graduation from the Sorbonne was at the Municipal School of Industrial Physics and Chemistry, where his older brother, Jacques, also worked. One of Pierre's early scientific accomplishments was to find a better way to measure heat wavelengths—the wavelengths of infrared light. Then, in 1880, he and Jacques discovered that certain **crystals**, when subjected to pressure, generate electricity; this effect they called "piezoelectricity." They also invented an electrometer, a device capable of measuring small amounts of electric current. Marie would later use this device in her investigations of radioactive materials.

After his brother married and moved away, Pierre began to focus his attention on the principle of magnetism, eventually showing that highly magnetic materials, called ferromagnetics, lose their magnetism at a certain temperature. This came to be known as the "Curie point."

Shown here is the electrometer invented by Pierre Curie and his older brother, Jacques. The device could measure precise electrical currents.

Indecision

Throughout the spring and into the early summer, the two like-minded scientists continued to see each other, becoming good friends. Pierre described his dream to Marie as "an existence entirely devoted to science," which echoed her own plans. Both had ruled out love and marriage in their lives—Marie because of the failed romance with Casimir Zorawski, and Pierre because his first love had died under mysterious circumstances. At the same time, the attraction between them continued to grow until it became clear their relationship was about more than just science.

By the time she was again preparing for her summer vacation in Poland, Pierre knew he wanted to marry Marie. Her feelings for him were equally strong, if not as openly expressed. Still, she held him off. She could not imagine leaving her beloved Poland permanently.

Almost as soon as she left Paris, Pierre began to write Marie letters. In the letters, he was careful always to refer to them as friends—perhaps afraid of pressuring her too much. While showing respect for her independence, it is clear he had begun to think of them as a couple. "We have promised each other— haven't we?—to be at least great friends," he wrote early in August that year. "It would be a fine thing . . . to pass our lives near each other hypnotized by our dreams, *your* patriotic dream, *our* humanitarian dream, and *our* scientific dream."

By autumn, Marie had made at least one important decision: to return to Paris to continue working on the study she had begun for Professor Lippmann. Her lodgings this year were once again courtesy of her sister Bronya, who had offered Marie a spare room adjoining her medical practice, which was utterly quiet after office

An undated photograph shows the devoted young couple, Pierre and Marie Curie.

hours were over for the day. It was here that Pierre continued his campaign to win her hand in marriage.

Ten more months would pass before Marie made up her mind to accept Pierre's proposal. It was not easy for her to turn her back on what she saw as her duty to her family and her country. Finally, though, she made her decision, confessing in a letter to her high school friend, Kazia, "It is a sorrow to me to have to stay forever in Paris, but what am I to do? Fate has made us deeply attached to each other and we cannot endure the idea of separating."

Fate had a great deal more in store for the shy but stubborn woman from Poland and the nonconformist dreamer from France, whose mutual idea of happiness was to share a life in science.

CHAPTER 4

Match Made in Science

*My husband and I were so closely united by our
affection and our common work that we passed
nearly all of our time together.*

M arie was ready when Pierre came to pick her up on that
beautiful summer day of July 26, 1895. Together they
traveled by train to his family's home in Sceaux, a village
outside Paris. There, in a simple, civil ceremony in the
town hall, Marie Sklodowska, dressed in a navy blue
woolen suit and a light blue blouse with stripes, wed Pierre
Curie. A small group was in attendance, just family and
friends close to the couple. For Marie, it was especially
important that her father and sister Hèla had made the trip
from Poland to share in her joy. The Dluskis—her sister
Bronya and brother-in-law Casimir—were, of course,
present, along with Pierre's family.

The party afterward, held in the Curie family's garden,
resembled more a picnic than a wedding reception. There,
amidst abundant summer flowers, the newlyweds shared
simple food—a turkey and fresh fruit—with their guests,
followed by boules (a sort of lawn bowling game) played
in the meadow near the Curies' property.

Honeymoon on Wheels

From Sceaux, the two nature lovers set off on a bicycle
tour of the northern part of the country. Their bicycles were
a wedding present to themselves, bought with the money

given to them by a cousin. They roamed the country roads more or less aimlessly, stopping where the beauty of the landscape caught their eyes or when they were tired. They lunched usually on bread, cheese, and fruit, and when night fell, stopped at inns they chanced upon along the way. They used no guidebooks, but only a compass to find their way; their few belongings were folded into leather satchels. Marie took charge of the little money they needed, which she kept in a leather belt around her waist, along with a knife and a watch.

During these weeks together, the couple solidified a friendship that had been growing for more than a year and marked the start of an uncommonly close-knit professional and romantic partnership. When they were not riding their bicycles, the two took long walks, and talked most often about their future work plans. Upon their return to Paris, Pierre

Marie and Pierre's honeymoon trip was the first of many they would take on their bicycles. Even in the city, whenever possible, they used their bikes to get around.

intended to take up his research on the mysterious growth of crystals, and he liked to brainstorm his ideas with Marie, who often followed behind him on the path, interrupting his train of thought only to offer suggestions. For her part, Marie had multiple goals: to earn a teaching certificate that would allow her

Nineteenth-Century Cycling

The Curies bought their bicycles at the height of the international bicycle craze in the 1890s—the "golden age" of bicycles. By the turn of the century, cycling clubs were forming around the globe, and touring and racing had become popular pastimes. Bicycles also began to take on greater practical importance. Just prior to the invention of the automobile, the foot-powered vehicles became one of the two primary modes of private transportation, along with horse-drawn carriages.

A French poster from the 1890s shows the latest craze in transportation—bicycles.

to teach in a girls' secondary school; to continue her study on the magnetic properties of steel for Professor Lippmann (work she now hoped to be able to do in the same laboratory as Pierre); and to take classes at the Sorbonne with the idea of one day preparing for her own doctoral studies.

When they were not riding their bicycles, the two took long walks, and talked most often about their future work plans.

Marie and Pierre ended their honeymoon trip in August in Chantilly, on a farm Bronya and Casimir had rented for the summer. There they met up again with Mr. Sklodowski and Hèla, who had stayed in France after the wedding.

Finally, though, the weather began to cool and the days to shorten. It was time to return to Paris and begin the work they had set out for themselves.

Two of a Kind

By October, the couple had moved into a fourth-floor walk-up at 24 **Rue** de la Glaciere, near the School of Physics and Chemistry, where Pierre was now a professor. This three-room apartment had little charm—its only redeeming feature was the view below of a garden, their bit of country in the city. On a tight budget, they furnished the apartment simply and sparsely, bringing in only what they needed.

Marie approached the management of their tiny household in the same way she did her studies and experiments. She kept notebooks on every aspect of their life, tracking each expense and purchase, in *His* and *Hers* columns. And although she learned to cook and had long known how to sew, she admitted she never mastered housekeeping, and these duties proved to be something of a trial for her.

After dinner, they usually retired to their shared study, where their desks faced each other. There they worked in companionable silence, often long into the night—just as

Marie Curie was known to keep detailed journals, noting with equal care the most intricate scientific experiments and the daily expenses of the Curies' personal life.

Marie had done throughout her student years. In fact, their home became more or less an extension of the professional spaces they worked in all day.

When not in class lecturing on electricity, Pierre could be found in an unused corner of the laboratory at the Physics School conducting his research on crystals. His supervisor eventually gave permission for Marie to work alongside him there, on her study of the magnetic properties of steel. "I thus learned from his example that one could work happily even in very insufficient quarters." (It was a lesson that would serve her well throughout her life, but never more so than in the next few years.)

Marie approached the management of their tiny household in the same way she did her studies and experiments.

At the same time Marie was working in the laboratory during this first year of her married life, she was also finishing up the course work she needed in order to teach physics to young girls at a secondary school. Not surprisingly, when the results were posted, Marie's name was at the top of the list. She and Pierre celebrated with another bicycle tour of another part of the French countryside.

Marie's certification meant the couple now had a dual source of regular income, which they would need more than ever, because she was pregnant with their first child.

Family Matters

Pregnancy would be something of a lesson in patience for Marie, who never before had allowed anything to interfere with her work and studies. Now, however, she had no choice, for she was quite sick throughout these months. Even though she looked forward to having a child, she admitted the ill effects brought on by the pregnancy were wearing her down, both physically and emotionally. In the spring, she wrote to her friend Kazia, "For more than two months I have had continual dizziness. . . . I feel unable to work and am in a very bad state of spirits."

At the same time, Pierre's mother, who had incurable breast cancer, was not expected to live much longer. Marie feared that Mrs. Curie's disease would "reach its end at the same time as my pregnancy. If this should happen, my poor Pierre will have some very hard weeks to go through." With pressure building, along with the heat in the city, Pierre insisted that Marie accept her father's invitation to join him in a little fishing village in Brittany, where he was spending the summer. Pierre would stay behind until the end of the school term and wait for his brother Jacques to arrive from Montpellier to take over helping their father care for Mrs. Curie.

This was Marie and Pierre's first separation since being married, and their letters reflected how much they missed each

A photograph of Marie Curie taken c. 1898.

other. He lamented that his "soul flew away" with her when she left. She was equally sad, telling him, "I expect you from morning to night and I don't see you coming."

In less than a month, they were reunited. Marie was now eight months pregnant, yet she convinced Pierre she felt well enough to go on one of their bicycle trips. The baby had other plans, however, forcing the pair to cut short their ride and rush back to Paris, where, on September 12, 1897, Irène Curie was born. Dr. Eugène Curie, Pierre's father, brought his six-pound, six-ounce granddaughter into the world.

The family's joy was subdued somewhat when, only two weeks later, Mrs. Curie died. Pierre had difficulty accepting her death, and it would be some time before he could even laugh without feeling guilty.

Working Mother

Pierre and Marie Curie were so similar in nature and so connected professionally that married life thus far had brought little change in the way Marie lived and worked. Motherhood, however, would prove to be a much more challenging adjustment for her. She admitted, "It became a serious problem how to take care of our little Irène and of our home without giving up my scientific work."

But this was a woman gifted at finding solutions to difficult problems, and her personal life was no different. To begin, they moved from their cramped quarters into a small, two-story house on Boulevard Kellermann on the outskirts of Paris. Shortly afterward, they asked Dr. Curie, Pierre's father, to join their household. The recent widower was only too glad to accept; in addition to easing his grief and loneliness, he felt he could be of use to the couple, now struggling to balance their work and home

Marie is shown here with her eldest daughter, Irène, who was born in 1897.

lives. They also hired a part-time nanny to help care for Irène, though often it was Dr. Curie who took responsibility for his granddaughter's care. Dr. Curie's reassuring presence also gave Marie, who frequently felt panicked about leaving her newborn daughter, the security she needed to again focus on her work.

Of this period, Marie would later write, "It was under this mode of quiet living, organized according to our desires, that we achieved the great work of our lives, work begun about the end of 1897 and lasting for many years."

t	a	d
[1]	[2]	[3]
<−200°	—	<0·05>
180°	—	0·59
(900°)	—	1·64
(1800°)	—	2·5
>(2500°)	—	<2·0 >
−203°	—	<0·7 >
<−200°	—	<1·0 >
96°	071	0·98
500°	027	1·74
600°	023	2·6
(1200°)	008	2·3
44°	128	2·2
114°	067	2·07
−75°	—	1·3
58°	084	0·87
(800°)	—	1·6
—	—	(2·5)
(2500°)	—	(5·1)
(2000°)	—	5·5
(2000°)	—	5·5
(1500°)	—	7·5
1400°	012	7·8
(1400°)	013	8·6
1350°	017	8·7
1054°	029	8·8
432°	—	7·1
30°	—	5·96
900°	—	5·47
500°	006	5·7
217°	—	4·8
−7°	—	3·1
39°	—	1·5
(600°)	—	2·5
—	—	(8·4)
(1500°)	—	4·1
(2000°)		
(1900°)		
1500°		
950°		
320°		
176°		
230°		
432°		
455°		
114°		
27°		
(600°)		
(700°)		
(800°)		
—		
(1500°)		
(2500°)		
2000°		
1775°		
1045°		
−39°		
294°	031	11·8
326°	029	11·3
268°	014	9·8
		11·1
(800°)	—	18·7

CHAPTER 5

New Science

Neither of us could foresee that in beginning this work we were to enter the path of a new science which we should follow for all our future.

Paris in the late 1890s was the capital city of the world—a leader in the arts, sciences, and technology. It was *the* place to be for writers, artists, political activists, and scientists. They all wanted to be part of the scene—a scene increasingly illuminated by the latest technological marvel, electricity. Day and night, these new-age thinkers could be found spilling onto the boulevards from sidewalk cafés, bars, dance halls, and theaters. Towering over the scene was the Eiffel Tower, the very symbol of innovation, built just two years before Marie Sklodowska-Curie arrived in 1891.

Marie and Pierre Curie rarely participated in this swirl of activities. Outside of work, she wrote, "We saw but a few friends, scientific workers, like ourselves, with whom we talked in our home or in our garden, while I did some sewing for my little girl." Yet even

The Eiffel Tower, the tallest building in the world until 1930, was the first to be lit entirely by electricity.

The Lumiere brothers, Auguste (left) and Louis (right), in 1895 discovered a way to turn photographs into moving pictures. Marie and Pierre Curie joined the crowds who stood in line to see the first movies.

these two workaholics could not help being distracted on occasion by the excitement of Paris. In particular, they enjoyed going to the theater; they were also among the hundreds who lined up for tickets to see the latest entertainment sensation, the *cinematographe*—the movies—developed in 1895 by two brothers, Auguste and Louis Lumiere, who had found a way to turn photographs into moving pictures.

Most of the time, however, Marie and Pierre Curie followed the same path, from home to their classrooms and to the laboratory, then back again each night. Pierre had settled on his objectives: In addition to his teaching duties, he was continuing his research on crystals. Marie was ready for a new challenge, for she had finished her study on the magnetic properties of steel for Professor Lippmann shortly before Irène was born. Her next goal, she decided, was to pursue her PhD in physics; and for that she would have to decide on a topic to study.

Chasing Rays

As a woman in the late nineteenth century, Marie Curie was at a distinct disadvantage to her male counterparts, but her timing could not have been better to embark on a career in science—and, particularly, in physics. The discoveries made at this time in history opened the door to modern physics and led

The work of Wilhelm Conrad Röntgen, who discovered X-rays in 1895, was a major influence on Marie's area of study.

to breakthroughs whose impact continues to be felt today. Marie Curie herself would walk through that door opened by two men in particular, Wilhelm Conrad Röntgen and Antoine Henri Becquerel, whose work laid the foundation for her own.

In 1895, Röntgen, a German physicist, discovered a new type of radiation while working on another experiment. Unlike ordinary light, this type of radiation could pass easily through some opaque substances, such as human flesh, while being stopped by other matter, such as metal or bone. That meant the rays could be used to see inside the human body. He called the mysterious phenomenon X-rays, the X standing for "the unknown"—he did not know their source. The scientific community went wild with enthusiasm upon learning of Röntgen's discovery, especially after seeing the first X-ray photographs.

Within months of Röntgen's discovery, a number of scientists began to study the association between X-rays and naturally occurring phosphorescence—the steady emission of light that follows exposure to some sort of radiation and continues for a time even after the radiation source is removed. They wanted to learn whether **fluorescent** bodies gave off other rays when exposed to light.

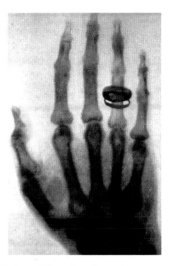

One of the earliest X-ray pictures, taken of the hand of Swiss scientist Alfred von Kolliker, January 23, 1896, clearly shows his ring.

One of those scientists was a French physicist, Henri Becquerel, whose own discovery, like Röntgen's, would be purely by chance. For his experiments, Becquerel was exposing uranium salts—chemical compounds formed from the element uranium and other substances—to sunlight. Then, during a stretch of cloudy weather, he found that the salts *emitted* rays spontaneously—even in the absence of an external source of energy, like the sun. This was yet another new type of radiation, one that could pass through metal foil and make an impression on a photographic plate surrounded by black paper. More, the rays caused the surrounding air to become a conductor of electricity—to *ionize* the air. What Becquerel did not know was that he was the first to witness spontaneous **radioactivity**. (Marie Curie would later invent the word *radioactivity* to describe this phenomenon.)

In comparison to X-rays, however, the so-called Becquerel rays generated much less interest in the science world. It was

This undated image shows Henri Becquerel's notes scribbled above the first evidence of radioactivity.

precisely that lack of interest, though, that sparked Marie Curie's curiosity. From her point of view, the situation was ideal, because she wanted to investigate something new. "My husband and I were much excited by this new phenomenon," she explained, "and I resolved to undertake the special study of it."

Prospecting for "Gold"

It was in the same spirit of adventure the prospectors must have felt during the Gold Rush that Marie Curie set out to find the source of this new ray. Like a prospector, she would spend years digging through tons of a dirt-like substance until she found her "gold," a chemical element that, like the precious yellow metal, also glowed to announce its presence. Unlike the prospectors, at

What Is Radiation?

Radiation is a natural part of our environment—there is no place in the universe where it does not exist. In the most basic sense, radiation is energy given off in the form of waves or small particles of matter; it exists whenever energy travels from one place to another.

There are many forms of radiation, some dangerous and some enormously helpful to humans. The most commonly known form is sunshine, whose rays are composed of photons (packets of energy). Sunshine is, on one hand, necessary to sustain life and to heat and light Earth. On the other hand, the ultraviolet rays of the Sun can cause sunburn and, worse, skin cancer. Other familiar forms of radiation are radio signals, which enable the transmission of sound; microwaves, which can cook food; and even the heat from a fire, which generates infrared radiation.

There are two main types of radiation: electromagnetic and particle (or particulate). Electromagnetic radiation comes from many sources; in fact, all materials that have been heated are sources of this type of radiation. Particle radiation comes from radioactive substances, such as uranium, radium, and other heavy elements found in rocks and soil; these are naturally radioactive. Radioactive forms of certain elements can also be created artificially in a laboratory.

the beginning of her adventure Marie had no idea what she was looking for, nor could she possibly have imagined it would take her years to coax it out of its hiding place.

Her first task, she knew, was to "measure the phenomenon with precision"; specifically, to measure the power of the rays that

A pensive Marie Curie poses in this undated photograph. In the late 1890s she was about to start her long search for the elusive radioactive elements.

caused the surrounding air to become a conductor of electricity. But how?

The answer was literally at her fingertips. The perfect tool was none other than the electrometer invented by her husband and his brother Jacques fifteen years earlier.

As important as *how* she would begin her research was *where* she could carry out this work. This question was more difficult to answer, and the solution much less satisfactory. The logical place to look was the Paris Municipal School of Industrial Physics and Chemistry, where Pierre was teaching and conducting his own research on crystals. His boss, the director of the school, eventually let Marie have the only space available: a small workshop on the ground floor of the school, currently being used for storage. It was here that Marie set up her equipment and began her experiments.

Within a few short weeks, she had uncovered a vital piece of information. In measuring the uranium rays emitted from the compounds (chemical substances made up of two or more elements) she was testing, she learned that the strength of the rays depended only on the amount of uranium in the compound. It was in no way affected by any other elements in the compounds, the form of the material (whether solid or powder, wet or dry), or by outside factors such as lighting or temperature. This was important because it told her that the radiation was a property of the uranium itself, a unique

Within a few short weeks, she had uncovered a vital piece of information.

characteristic of the metal. That realization led to the next question she wanted to investigate: Were there any other chemical elements that also emitted this radiation?

The next step, she decided, was "to examine all known chemical bodies, either in their pure state or in compounds." By April 1898, she had the result of this work: Among all those bodies, the only ones known to emit rays similar to those of uranium were in compounds containing thorium, another radioactive element. This information gave her the next important clue in solving the mystery of the rays. She knew she should stop working with inactive minerals and concentrate on **ores**, minerals or rocks, that contained both uranium and thorium. One of those was called pitchblende, a brownish-black mineral rich in uranium. Traditionally, pitchblende had been mined to extract its uranium content, which was used to color glass and ceramic

A card, dated c. 1916, depicts the mining of pitchblende, the ore in which Marie Curie found both polonium and radium.

WILLS'S CIGARETTES.

MINING PITCHBLENDE.

glazes and to tint photographs (color photography had not yet been invented). Once stripped of most of its uranium, the mineral was regarded as worthless and discarded. It was in that "waste" that Marie would find what she was looking for.

Hitting Pay Dirt

In February 1898, Marie found that pitchblende gave off radiation four times greater than could be explained by the remaining uranium content in the pitchblende. This was so surprising that she thought she must have made some mistake in her measurements. She conducted the same experiment over and over, always coming up with the same result. Finally, she could no longer question what she had found and what it meant. Her excitement was apparent in a letter she wrote to Bronya: "The radiation that I couldn't explain comes from a new chemical element. The element is there and I've got to find it. We are sure!"

An important shift is contained in that letter, for the *we* indicates that Marie was no longer working alone on the project. Pierre had become so excited by his wife's findings that he abandoned his own research (temporarily, he thought at the time) to help her. She would need his help, for pitchblende contains as

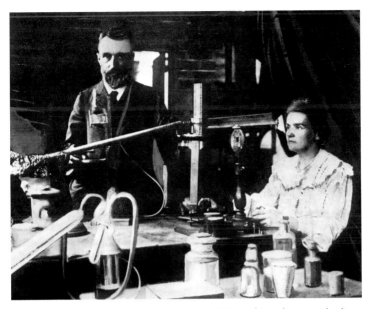
Pierre and Marie Curie worked side by side in their lab to isolate polonium and radium.

many as thirty different chemical elements, making it difficult to find the mysterious new one she suspected was there.

Determined to leave nothing to chance, in June 1898 the Curies added a third member to their team, Gustave Bémont, a chemist and laboratory chief at the school where Pierre worked. Bémont suggested the process they would use: First, grind the pitchblende into a powder, then dissolve it in acid, over and over, to separate all the different elements contained within the pitchblende. Each time they repeated the process, Marie became more convinced that there was something in the pitchblende more radioactive than uranium.

Finally, they had a batch whose only known component besides uranium was bismuth, a heavy, brittle metallic element. When she tested it, she was astonished to discover it contained something that was one hundred fifty times more radioactive than uranium. Further tests, removing more and more bismuth, resulted in higher and higher levels of radioactivity in the concentrated bismuth sample. Now there could be no doubt: They had discovered a new element.

Marie named it *polonium*, in honor of the country of her birth.

All along, the Curies had kept the scientific community informed of their progress in the standard method of the day: by writing research papers and delivering them to the members of the prestigious French Academy of Sciences. However, neither Pierre nor Marie was a member of this exclusive society, so they were not allowed to read their own reports. Instead, they had to ask colleagues who were members to do it for them. It was Henri Becquerel who read the Curies' joint report, titled, "On a New Radioactive Substance Contained in Pitchblende." The title marked the first time the word *radioactive* was used.

Seeing Is Believing

It was only the beginning, for Marie now suspected there was a second new element in the pitchblende. But the search for it would have to wait. It was time for the *grande vacances*—summer vacation—when the French close up shop and head for the countryside. The Curies, with their ten-month-old toddler and her grandfather, joined the throngs of Parisian families escaping the heat and humidity of the city.

Come September they were back in the lab, refreshed and intent on finding the second element. With Bémont at their sides, they again began to remove all the elements from a new batch of pitchblende, this time leaving only uranium and barium, another known element. In this sample, Marie realized, was another substance, one much more radioactive than uranium and even

As an associate of the French Academy of Sciences, physicist Henri Becquerel presented the Curies' findings to its members.

polonium (now known to be approximately one million times more active than uranium). "In December, 1898," she later wrote, "we could announce the discovery of this new and now famous element, to which we gave the name of radium."

The news, however, was greeted with little excitement by scientists, who require proof of every claim. It would take the Curies four years of hard labor to provide that proof, which had to be given in terms of the **atomic weight** of the new substances.

Elements and Compounds

The reason the possibility of identifying a new chemical element was so exciting to the Curies was that, at the time, scientists did not have a clear-cut way of determining whether a substance was an entirely new element (which contains only one kind of atom) or a compound (a blend) of already-known elements. Each element has an atomic weight, determined by the number of protons (positively charged particles) and neutrons (uncharged particles) in the nucleus (the core) of the atom.

Everything in the world is composed of chemical elements that are made up of atoms, which combine in countless ways. Probably the most well-known compound is H_2O, water. It contains two elements—two atoms of hydrogen (indicated by the 2) and one atom of oxygen. Scientists of the Curies' day also wanted to understand why atoms from different elements, when combined, behaved as they did. Why, for example, did oxygen combine with hydrogen to produce a liquid?

Chemical elements are categorized and arranged according to their atomic weights in the Periodic Table of Elements, devised in the late 1860s by Dmitri Mendeleev (1834–1907), a Russian chemist. At that time, sixty-three elements were known to exist. Where a gap existed in the table, he predicted a new element would be found. Polonium, the Curies' first new element, was given the number 84; radium became number 88. Today, there are more than a hundred elements in the Periodic Table of Elements.

This is an early version of Dmitri Mendeleev's Periodic Table of Elements, which does not contain the Curies' discoveries, polonium and radium.

CHAPTER 6

Something Out of Nothing

We had no money, no suitable laboratory,
no personal help for our great and difficult
undertaking. It was like creating something
out of nothing.

Before the Curies could even begin to approach the final
stage in proving polonium and radium existed, they first
had to find a large enough supply of pitchblende to test,
and then find a larger space in which to work on it.

The first task was particularly problematic, for
pitchblende in its original form (with uranium still in it)
was very expensive—way beyond the means of the Curies,
who were just making ends meet on their teaching salaries.
After trying to locate sources all over the world, they
learned that great heaps of waste pitchblende (with most of
its uranium content stripped from it) lay on the forest floor
outside the town of St. Joachimsthal in Bohemia (now part
of the Czech Republic), where it had been dumped by
workers from a nearby uranium mine.
Marie suspected it still might contain
sufficient traces of the metal for
their purposes. With the help

Who would have thought this black
rock of pitchblende contains the
element that would open the door
to the atomic age?

of an Austrian colleague, they began to negotiate for the purchase of this "secondhand" pitchblende.

At the same time, they began to search for more adequate laboratory space. Once again, Pierre approached the director of the School of Physics. Though willing to help, he had nothing suitable to offer, but told them they were welcome to use the abandoned shed across the courtyard from the room where Marie had been working. The building had once served as a dissecting lab for medical students and, later, as storage for unwanted odds and ends from the school. The roof leaked; the walls, too. It contained little furniture beyond some creaky, cracked wooden tables and benches, a blackboard, and a cast-iron stove. It would be difficult to imagine a more inappropriate place to conduct the kind of precise experiments Marie and Pierre had outlined. Yet it

An undated photograph shows the "miserable old shed" where radium was discovered. Today, five small concrete pillars in a parking lot outline where the building once stood.

was "in this miserable old shed," she later wrote, that they would pass "the best and happiest years of our life."

With the keys to this makeshift laboratory in hand, they waited anxiously to hear about the pitchblende. Fortunately, the strings being pulled on their behalf came together: The Austrian government, which owned the uranium mine, agreed to let the two scientists have a ton of the residue ore just for the cost of transporting it. And if they wanted more later, they would be able to get it at low cost.

Finally, they could get to work.

Working to Isolate Radium

A heavy wagon, like those used to deliver coal, pulled up to the small building on Rue l'Homond one morning early in 1899, weighed down with sacks containing what appeared to be nothing more than dirt mixed with pine needles. What in those sacks, the driver of the truck must have wondered, could cause such excitement in the woman in the white laboratory coat hurrying out to meet him?

Barely had the first string-tied bags been unloaded before Marie tore one open and plunged her hands into the gritty stuff. It was *her* pitchblende, and in it, she was sure, radium was hidden. She was determined to extract it, "even if she had to treat a mountain of this **inert** stuff . . ."

Marie and Pierre Curie would, in fact, have to go through a mountain of the "inert stuff"—literally, tons of it—before they were able to isolate her mysterious glowing element.

In this shed, which itself would become famous as the site where radium was "born," the Curies began the exhausting process of isolating the element. Within the first year, the pair decided it would be easier to separate radium than polonium, due to its stronger radioactivity, and so they focused their efforts on this element alone. They also realized they would be able to cover ground more quickly if they separated their individual efforts.

Pierre, with his expertise in building and working with delicate instruments, concentrated on trying to solve the questions posed by radioactivity itself. Marie chose to take on the part of the process that was the most physically demanding: the actual separation of

It was her pitchblende, and in it, she was sure, radium was hidden.

the radium from the pitchblende. Batch by batch, in a giant iron cauldron she stirred her "stew" of pitchblende mixed with chemicals, all the while breathing in the fumes they were giving off (the shed did not have proper ventilation of any kind). "Sometimes," she wrote, "I had to spend a whole day mixing a boiling mass with a heavy iron rod nearly as large as myself. I would be broken with fatigue at the day's end." Other days, she performed a delicate technique called **fractional crystallization** used in chemistry to obtain very pure substances.

At least the hard work helped take her mind off the fact that Bronya, her sister and best friend, had recently

An undated photograph shows Marie Curie holding flasks containing various chemicals used in the process to isolate radium.

moved back to Poland, where she and her husband planned to open an experimental **sanatorium** in the Carpathian Mountains for tuberculosis patients, the disease that had killed their mother.

Life Outside the Lab

Although her sister's absence sometimes made her feel lonely and cut off from her Polish roots, most days Marie was too busy to dwell on it. Due in part to a number of papers Marie and Pierre had published between 1899 and 1900 on their work, their reputation had begun to grow throughout Europe—though, ironically, less so in France. One result was that in 1900 Pierre was offered a very well-paid professorship by the University of Geneva in Switzerland; Marie, too, was offered a position at the school. Though accepting these jobs would have increased their income dramatically, they feared the change would interrupt and delay their experimental work, so they decided to stay in Paris.

Earlier in the year, they had moved from their apartment near the Sorbonne to a two-story house at 108 Boulevard Kellermann, where they had more room, a terrace, and a garden. The fresh air and quieter neighborhood were better for Irène, now three, and Pierre's aging father. It also became a refuge for Marie and Pierre. Both noticed that their health had begun to deteriorate. Pierre had begun to experience serious pain in his legs, which sometimes kept him—and the frightened Marie—up at night. Marie was not well, either: She had been losing weight and had started sleepwalking. Both were constantly exhausted. They blamed overwork and poor diet for their problems. Today, it is believed that these were the first signs the Curies were suffering from exposure to megadoses of radioactivity.

To help ease their financial situation, both took on new teaching jobs. Pierre became an assistant professor at the

In a c. 1901 photograph, Marie, Irène, and Pierre Curie stand in the garden of their home on Boulevard Kellermann.

Sorbonne, and Marie became a part-time teacher at a school for young girls in Sevres, a suburb of the city. It was another of her firsts—no other woman had ever taught there. She got off to a rough start, however. She intimidated her first students by talking too fast and over their heads due to nervousness. Soon she relaxed and became a favorite among them. She supported their desire to learn science and gave them confidence in their abilities to master the material; she also allowed them to handle the physics apparatus, which their male teachers had never permitted.

Deadly Gas

As they worked to isolate radium, the Curies did not know they were breathing in the fumes of a deadly gas. A year after the Curies announced the discovery of polonium and radium, Ernest Rutherford, a physicist from New Zealand, discovered another chemical element, radon. Today, radon—a gas that cannot be seen and has no smell or taste—is known to be a deadly poison, which can accumulate in buildings and homes. According to the U.S. Environmental Protection Agency, radon is a leading cause of lung cancer today, killing approximately 20,000 people every year.

Ernest Rutherford was the New Zealand physicist who discovered the deadly gas radon.

Marie Curie is surrounded by her students at the school in Sevres. She soon became a favorite among the girls by supporting their desire to study physics.

In other ways, too, things began to look up for the hardworking couple. A physicist named Georges Sagnac began helping out in their lab. They also received some financial aid in 1902, most notably from the French Academy of Sciences, which awarded them a grant for twenty thousand francs (worth approximately $4,000 at the time). With this money they bought more of the waste pitchblende and hoped that from it they would be able to produce a large enough sample of pure radium to estimate its atomic weight.

Proof Positive

"At last the time came," Marie wrote, "when the isolated substances showed all the characteristics of a pure chemical body"—it was composed of a single compound. In late March,

The light given off by the radium in this dish makes it possible to read the card placed above it.

she took her precious sample to a man named Eugene Demarcay, an expert in spectroscopy, a method used to help identify mystery elements. At first he had trouble working with the sample. It was so radioactive that it threw his electric equipment off-kilter. Still, he kept at it until finally he was able to tell Marie that the radium sample weighed a little more than one-tenth of a gram; from this Marie calculated its atomic weight at 225.93.

She had it! "It had taken me almost four years," she wrote, "to produce the kind of evidence which chemical science demands, that radium is truly a new element. . . . The demonstration that cost so much effort was the basis of the new science of radioactivity."

Over time, many others would have much more to say about this momentous discovery. Years later, a friend and colleague would compare the discovery of radium to the discovery of fire.

Radium

Radium, number 88 on the Periodic Table of Elements, is the heaviest of the alkaline earth metals—silver-colored, soft metals. It is a good conductor of electricity and is intensely radioactive. When newly cut, it has a brilliant white color; when exposed to air, it turns black; in the dark, it glows with an eerie blue-green light. When purified as a chloride (a chemical compound containing chlorine), it looks like white powder or table salt. Radium also spontaneously gives off heat. Its radioactivity is "contagious," causing anything near it to become radioactive as well.

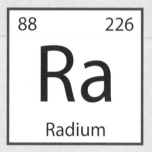

In the Periodic Table, the element radium, designated as Ra, is shown as atomic number 88, with an atomic weight of 226.

And one of the many biographers of Marie Curie would write that confirmation of the existence of radium signaled the birth of atomic energy and that it was the key to unlocking the mystery of the composition of the universe.

Marie wasted no time in writing to her father in Warsaw to tell him the good news, hoping it would cheer him during his recovery from injuries he had sustained when he was hit by a streetcar. He wrote back congratulating her on her accomplishment, but added it was a pity her work seemed to have no practical value. Sadly, he would not live to learn how wrong he was, that his youngest daughter's discovery would have value beyond counting. On May 14, 1902, Wladislaw Sklodowski died after undergoing gall bladder surgery. Marie had been on her way home to see him when it happened, and it broke her heart that she did not get to see him alive one more time.

True to her nature, Marie coped with her grief by throwing herself back into her work. Her primary goal now was to finish writing her dissertation, an extensive report describing the results of her research. Then she would defend her findings in front of a committee of three professors. These were the final requirements necessary to obtain her PhD.

On that day she would be walking onto the world stage, where over the next few years she would be praised and admired but also criticized and scorned—the double-edged sword that so often is the curse of celebrity.

CHAPTER 7

Reluctant Celebrities

[T]he invasion of publicity . . . the overturn of our voluntary isolation was a cause of real suffering for us, and had all the effect of disaster.

It was standing room only in the students' hall at the Sorbonne on June 25, 1903, the day Marie Sklodowska-Curie was scheduled to defend her dissertation. The buzz of anticipation traveled around the room like a warm breeze, and as more and more students, scientists, and members of the public began to crowd the space it began to heat up, making the crowd increasingly impatient. Among them at the back, were Pierre, Bronya, and Dr. Curie, as well as close friends and colleagues and a group from the girls' school in Sevres.

At last Marie entered the room via a hidden winding staircase to present herself to the formally dressed committee of professors sitting at the long table at the front of the room. They had already read her dissertation, "Researches on Radioactive Substances," and they would now ask her a final series of

This is the cover of Marie Sklodowska-Curie's PhD dissertation, titled "Researches on Radioactive Substances."

questions to determine whether she had successfully completed the requirements to earn her PhD.

Did she, as she was entering the hall, think back on the young, terrified girl of so many years ago standing in front of the Russian inspector at Madame Sikorska's school? Was she aware of the crowd? On this day, wearing the new black dress Bronya had convinced her she must buy for this important occasion, she moved calmly to the blackboard, where she spoke softly, sometimes illustrating in chalk her answers to the questions posed by the committee.

With the last question asked and answered, the three professors took a few minutes to discuss her responses. Then Dr. Gabriel Lippmann, Marie's advisor and one of her first professors, made the announcement: "The University of Paris [the Sorbonne] accords you the title of doctor of physical science with the mention *tres honorable* [high honors]." The committee also told Marie she had produced the "greatest scientific contribution ever made in a doctoral thesis."

The committee also told Marie she had produced the "greatest scientific contribution ever made in a doctoral thesis."

The crowd could be contained no longer. Upon hearing those words, they burst into applause as if having just seen a great performance. And so they had. They had witnessed a major event in academic history: the first woman ever to be awarded a PhD in France and in a field of study considered a man's world.

Dark Signs in the Light

As they had following their marriage ceremony, the Curies and their family and friends gathered for an informal, backyard celebration of Marie's remarkable achievement, this time at the house on Kellermann. It had been arranged by Paul Langevin, a former student of Pierre's and now colleague and good friend to both the Curies. Sitting outside in the warm night, Pierre entertained the guests with a sort of show-and-tell, producing a tube of radium salt in solution.

Almost immediately the tube began to glow, lighting up the darkness to everyone's delight. Scientist Ernest Rutherford noticed something disturbing at the same time: In the glow given off by the radium, he could see clearly that Pierre's hand was red, raw, and sore, and it was shaking so much that he had trouble holding on to the tube. Georges Sagnac, one of the Curies' lab helpers, was so upset that night by Marie's weakened appearance, he later wrote Pierre a ten-page letter expressing his concern.

Two months later, Marie herself could no longer ignore the state of her health when in August she lost the child she was then carrying, five months into the pregnancy. She blamed herself for using up her strength, writing to Bronya, "I regret this bitterly, as I have paid dearly for it." Her sadness was compounded when soon after, Bronya lost her second son to meningitis.

A photo of Marie and Pierre Curie shows them enjoying the outdoors in one of their rare breaks from lab work.

Throughout the summer, Marie continued to feel sick, though she regained some of her strength while on vacation with the family. Back in Paris in September, she became ill again, now with flu-like symptoms and a bad cough. Her doctor also told her she had anemia—her blood was not producing enough red cells, causing intense weakness and fatigue.

In the coming weeks, the state of the Curies' health would become more of an issue, for the couple was about to be tested in a way neither could have imagined.

The High Price of Fame

Since they had announced the discovery of polonium and radium, the Curies were in demand to make appearances to explain their work; they were also being singled out for honors and awards. In June 1903, not long before Marie had earned her PhD, both Curies had gone to London as guests of the Royal Institution of Great Britain, the oldest independent research organization in the world. Women were not allowed to speak at the institution, so Pierre alone gave the lecture, being sure to stress Marie's critical role in their work. As she sat in the front row listening, no doubt she was more concerned about his health than what he was saying. What the audience did not know was that Pierre had been so weak before the lecture that he could hardly dress himself; and only Marie knew that the reason he spilled some radium during his demonstration was that his hands were so unsteady. (More than half a century later, certain surfaces in the lecture hall were found to still be radioactive and had to be cleaned.)

Five months later in early November, the couple was awarded an important prize from the Royal Society of London, the Humphry Davy Medal, given every year to the most important

Shown here is a modern-day picture of the Royal Institution of Great Britain lecture hall, in London. More than fifty years after Pierre Curie spilled some radium while giving a lecture there in 1903, some surfaces were still found to be radioactive.

discovery in chemistry. Marie was too sick to attend, so Pierre returned alone to London to accept the award.

Then on November 14, they received a letter informing them they had been awarded the Nobel Prize in Physics, together with Henri Becquerel. In that moment, their lives changed—for better and worse. The honor was, of course, a great one; and they were thankful for the prize money (split equally with Becquerel). The seventy thousand francs they received (approximately $20,000) was "a great help in the continuation of our researches."

But the Nobel Prize brought with it something the Curies did not expect, did not want, and did not know how to handle: fame. They became the pop stars of their time, with the media and the public hungry for every detail of their story. Everywhere, they

The Curies' Nobel Prize

The Nobel Prize, established by Swedish scientist Alfred Nobel, was first awarded in 1901 in five categories: physics, chemistry, physiology or medicine, literature, and peace.

Few today realize that Marie Curie, the first woman to receive a Nobel Prize, almost did not. Four members of the French Academy of Science made a determined effort to keep Marie's name off the list of nominees. They sent a letter to the selection committee in which they gave Pierre sole credit for his and Marie's work. Two of these men knew full well that Marie deserved to win the prize as much as Pierre: her former professors, Gabriel Lippmann and Henri Poincaré.

Why? Many believe it was sexism, pure and simple. Others say it was the French prejudice against foreigners. Fortunately, a Swedish mathematician on the nominating committee who supported women in the sciences stepped in, preventing the injustice.

In 1903, Marie Curie became the first woman to win a Nobel Prize—an honor she shared with her husband, Pierre, and Henri Becquerel.

The high price of fame: In an undated photograph, Marie Curie is shown being chased by photographers.

were pursued by reporters. Even six-year-old Irène and the family cat were put under the media microscope.

Pierre in particular suffered from the constant distractions. As his productivity dropped, his anger grew. He apologized to a good friend for not writing, saying, "[I]t is because of the stupid life I am leading just now. You have seen this sudden fad for radium. . . . We have been pursued by the journalists and photographers of every country on earth; they have even gone so far as to reproduce my daughter's conversation with her nurse and to describe the black-and-white cat we have at home."

An Industry Is Born

Pierre was right to call the interest in radium a fad, and it was catching on everywhere. Long before both the power—and dangers—of radium could be fully investigated and understood, scientists from all over the world began clamoring for information about the element, especially when it was found to have the potential to heal cancerous tumors. From as early as 1900, they began to bombard the Curies with requests for details about the process they used to prepare pure radium. Not far behind were business entrepreneurs of the day who were anxious to take advantage of the public fascination with radium's luminous properties. They proposed making such products as face cream, guaranteed to give women's skin a healthy glow; radium-glow nail polish; hair tonics, promising to permanently curl hair; even luminescent clothing, a favorite among stage performers.

The Curies were now faced with a big decision: Should they patent their discoveries and processes? A patent would give them the exclusive right to take advantage of their work, either by developing moneymaking commercial applications themselves or by licensing others to do so in return for a fee. The answer seemed obvious: Taking out a patent would end their financial worries forever and secure the future for their family. Like many scientists of the day, however, Marie and Pierre

A 1924 advertisement promotes a permanent hair-waving product containing radium.

believed strongly that scientific discoveries should be made available at no charge, for the good of the general public. In particular, they were confident radium would find important uses in the world of medicine and wanted to encourage its development in this field.

A Daughter Is Born

The Curies did not attend the Nobel Prize ceremony held a month after the announcement of their award. Pierre wrote to the secretary of the Academy of Science of Stockholm saying that they could not get away because of their teaching duties, adding that Marie had been ill all summer and was not yet fully recovered. It would be more than a year before they would make the trip to Sweden for the award presentation.

Fortunately, they did not have to wait a year to receive their prize money. On January 2, 1904, it was deposited in their bank account, and immediately the Curies began to take steps

. . . Marie and Pierre believed strongly that scientific discoveries should be made available at no charge, for the good of the general public.

to make their daily lives less stressful. Pierre gave up teaching his classes at the School of Physics, and they hired an assistant in the laboratory; at home, Marie hired a maid and a cook to help with the housekeeping. The money could do nothing, though, to stop the intrusions by the press and the public.

Over the next weeks, Marie's mood continued to darken. Even learning in March that she was going to have a baby failed to raise her spirits. She feared she might lose this baby, too, due to her exhaustion and poor health. Wisely, she finally asked for time off from her teaching duties and stopped working at the laboratory.

Marie and Pierre are pictured with daughter Irène in 1904, shortly before daughter Ève was born.

Nevertheless, even after the birth of a healthy daughter—beautiful black-haired, blue-eyed Ève—on December 6, 1904, Marie remained very depressed.

It would take a visit from Bronya and several weeks of rest before Marie began to feel like herself again. An unmistakable sign of improvement was her desire to return to the laboratory and to teaching. In February she was back at work, though still worrying how she would handle everything. "I have a great deal of work," she wrote to her brother, "what with the housekeeping, the children, the teaching, and the laboratory, and I don't know how I shall manage it all."

With the coming of spring, however, both Marie and Pierre were in better spirits, and by June 1905 they felt well enough to make their long-delayed trip to Stockholm, where Pierre would deliver the Nobel lecture. As he had in London, he made sure to highlight Marie's role in their work, mentioning her name ten times. Looking back, his speech was memorable for another important reason: In it, he seemed to be sending a warning of the possible dangers of radium. "It can even be thought that radium could become very dangerous in criminal hands, and here the question can be raised whether mankind benefits from knowing the secrets of nature."

It seemed a passing thought, though, and if he made the connection from his words to the deterioration of his health, he never said so—at least not in public.

On the return from their successful trip to Sweden, the Curies left for their long summer vacation in a quiet village not far from Paris. A farmhouse there had become a second home to the family in recent years. This year, especially, they needed the rest, for the fall promised to be just as hectic. Even the eight-year-old Irène had a busy schedule. She was in school all morning and in the afternoons took gymnastics, drawing, and music classes and was learning to speak Polish.

Back in Paris in September, it was business as usual for all the work-minded Curies.

Then, in mid-April, everything changed.

CHAPTER 8

Facing the Future Alone

*Crushed by the blow, I did not feel able to face
the future.*

It was raining in Paris on Thursday, April 19, 1906, and it
was a little stormy inside the Curie home as well. Marie
was taking care of her daughters, now nine and two. On his
way out the door, Pierre called upstairs to her, asking—not
for the first time—when she would be joining him at the
lab. Somewhat irritated now, she told him she had no idea
and begged him not to torment her. Those were the last
words she would speak to her husband.

Pierre left, heading first to his laboratory to get in a
couple hours of work before leaving to attend a meeting
of the Association of Professors of the
Science Faculties. It was after two when
the meeting ended and still the rain was
coming down. Next on his schedule
was a stop at his publisher's office,
where he planned to check the proofs
of his latest article. Hunching under
his big, black umbrella, he set off. He
arrived to find the door locked—the
workers had gone on strike, a fairly
common occurrence in France.

Pierre Curie is shown in a photograph taken
January 1906, just months before his death.

On he went to his next stop, the library at the French Institute. Walking along Rue Dauphine, a notoriously narrow street, he had to jostle for space among the sea of umbrellas, sometimes walking along the curb, other times stepping into the street in order to make headway. Nearing the institute, he had to cross one of the busiest, most dangerous intersections in Paris. On a good day, it was difficult; on a day like this, it was next to impossible. Pierre, probably deep in thought as always, and perhaps forgetting for a moment the trouble he had been having with his legs, stepped out into traffic and began to hurry across the street.

Suddenly, he found himself trapped between a tram and a horse-drawn wagon carrying several tons of cargo. He grabbed on to the chest of the horse closest to him to try to keep from falling, but both animals reared up and he lost his grip. The driver of the wagon pulled with all his might to turn away from the man who had just gone down in front of him. He almost succeeded. The front wheels missed Pierre entirely, but the momentum of the vehicle could not be stopped in time, and the back left wheel struck the head of Pierre Curie. He was killed instantly.

Going on Alone

It was Dr. Curie, Pierre's father, home with Ève, who learned of the accident first. He knew immediately from the look on the faces of the two men who had rung the doorbell. He said, "My son is dead."

Together, the three men sat down to wait for Marie. At around six she came in with Irène, and both were in high spirits from a day out together. Disbelief then shock came over her as she tried to grasp what she had just been told. She did not cry—not then.

She sent Irène to their neighbors, checked on Ève, then sat down in silence to wait with the others for her husband's body to be brought to the house.

It was not until the next day, with the arrival of Pierre's brother, Jacques, from Montpellier, that Marie gave way to overpowering grief. She was able to compose herself only to check on her daughters from time to time. She had not yet told Irène her father was dead, at first telling her he had hurt his head; Ève, she knew, was too young to understand.

On Saturday, Pierre was buried in the family plot in the cemetery in Sceaux. It was a quiet ceremony, exactly as Pierre

It was not until the next day . . . that Marie gave way to overpowering grief.

would have wanted, though Marie and Jacques were not entirely successful at keeping away a crowd of people wanting to express their condolences. Naturally, reporters invaded, some hiding among headstones in the cemetery to get the story.

In the days and weeks that followed, the tributes to Pierre came in a constant flow, as constant as Marie's flow of tears. She could not be comforted. Not even her sister and brother, Bronya and Jòzef, who had hurried from Poland to be with her, could break through the wall of sorrow that had descended on their baby sister. Marie had learned early how to cope with the loss of those she loved most in the world. But this was Pierre, the love of her life, her best friend and professional partner, and the father of her daughters. How could she go on without him? How could anyone expect it?

The answer lay in those two words: *her daughters.* Irène, in particular, would need her now. So much like her father and already showing signs of great skill in science and mathematics, she would miss him most. When told of her father's death on the

Marie is shown with daughters Irène and Ève after Pierre was killed.

Sunday following his burial, she did not understand at first. Later she cried, and for a time was afraid to speak of him.

It was with her daughters' futures in mind that Marie went back to work. And it was her well-known pride and determination that led her to refuse the government's offer of a pension—financial support—for her and the children. "I'm young enough to earn my living and that of my children," she said.

Painful Honor

Gradually, Marie began spending more time each day in the laboratory; and when the question arose at the Sorbonne as to who should replace Pierre, the answer seemed obvious. But allow a woman to teach at the Sorbonne? Many strongly objected to the idea. The solution was to give Marie the job but without the official title. On May 14, barely a month after Pierre's accident, it was announced that Marie would take over his teaching duties at the Sorbonne. Her feelings, understandably, were mixed: "The honor that now came to me was deeply painful under the cruel circumstances of its coming. Besides, I wondered whether I would be able to face such a grave responsibility."

The announcement of her first lecture, to be given November 5, 1906, was front-page news. Before noon that day, a

In an undated photograph, Marie, wearing her usual black dress, is seated in a familiar place—her lab.

crowd began gathering at the entrance gate to the Sorbonne. When the doors to the lecture hall opened, the two hundred seats were filled instantly, leaving standing room only. Even the students enrolled in the course had trouble finding space among the reporters, photographers, and "celebrity watchers" from all walks of life—most of whom did not know the first thing about physics or about Marie's work.

To the expectant crowd, it was an event; to the grieving widow, it was an ordeal. Entering quietly and setting her watch down on the table in front of her, she began: "When one considers the progress that has been made in physics in the past ten years, one is surprised at the advance that has taken place in our ideas concerning electricity and matter." It was

A drawing of Marie captures her lecturing at the Sorbonne, the first woman to do so.

exactly the point at which Pierre had ended his last lecture and marked the beginning of Marie's life without him.

Establishing a Routine

As much for herself as for Irène and Ève, for the next couple of years Marie sought to establish calm in all their lives. She moved them to a small house in Sceaux. There she could be nearer to Pierre's grave, give Irène and Ève greater access to the outdoors, and enable Dr. Curie to live out his days in the village where he had raised his own family.

She joined the daily commuters to Paris on the train platform every morning around eight, leaving her daughters in the care of their loving grandfather and a Polish governess. A half hour later she was in the laboratory on Rue Cuvier, the one given too late to Pierre but now being put to good use by his wife.

In 1907, Andrew Carnegie, the American steel tycoon, donated an annual income of $50,000 for scholarships, allowing her to expand her laboratory staff of student researchers—many of them young women—to help with her ongoing investigations of radium, polonium, and radioactivity. (Polonium would prove much more difficult than radium to pin down in terms of numbers, because it decays very rapidly and has many different forms; it is also highly toxic—poisonous.) She interrupted her work there only to teach her classes, still at the girls' school in

Pierre Curie's Legacy

Because he gave up his own research to help Marie with hers and then died so young, Pierre Curie's scientific achievements today are chiefly linked with those of his wife. However, the modern world owes much to the earlier work of Pierre—and his brother, Jacques. The piezoelectric crystals they discovered are today used in such devices as sonar equipment, microphones, electronic igniters, and the buzzers used in cell phones and pagers.

Sevres and at the Sorbonne. In 1908, she was finally given the official title of full professor at the Sorbonne, and she was now teaching the first course ever offered in radioactivity.

She also took it upon herself to make sure Irène and Ève received a well-rounded education, just as her parents had done for the Sklodowski children. She had inherited her parents' strong views on teaching

In 1908, she was finally given the official title of full professor . . .

and did not entirely approve of the French school system, which she felt put too much emphasis on class work and not enough on physical exercise and creativity.

With the help of some like-minded friends from the university, she organized a "cooperative group for the education of our children, each of us taking charge of the teaching of a particular subject to all of the young people." It was reminiscent of the Flying University of her youth, though classes did not have to be conducted in secret. The arrangement lasted for two years and

Marie and her daughters, Ève and Irène, stand in the garden of their home in Sceaux. At far left is a classmate of Irène's from the cooperative school.

was, in her mind, a success. At that point, Irène had to be enrolled in the government school system so she could earn the official certificate required to enroll in college. She was given advanced placement upon returning to the French classroom, which later enabled her to begin her scientific studies at the Sorbonne ahead of her age group.

In the four years since Pierre had died, Marie had succeeded in regaining her equilibrium, if not her joy in life. The price she was paying, however, was high. Leaving home early every day and coming home late most nights, she grew increasingly tired and her health began to deteriorate steadily.

Still, her successes began to mount, and her fame continued to grow. Once again she would find herself at the mercy of the media. Beginning in 1910, she would learn just how quickly and cruelly it could turn, tearing down the reputation of one it had spent so much time building up.

In the Shadow of Success

My candidacy [for the Academy of Sciences] provoked a vivid public interest, especially because it involved the question of the admission of women to the Academy.

It was a letter to the editor appearing in the *London Times* fewer than four months after Pierre was killed that reawakened Marie's passion for work and fueled her drive to defend the work she and Pierre had accomplished in the last eight years. The letter was, essentially, an attack on that work, and its author was one of Pierre's admirers—Lord Kelvin. Born William Thomson, Lord Kelvin was famous for developing the Kelvin scale, a measure of absolute temperature, and was considered England's greatest scientist.

In the letter, Kelvin wrote that the Curies had been mistaken in claiming radium as a new element; it was, he said, a compound of helium and lead. Though few took this challenge seriously—Kelvin had once called

Shown is an undated photograph of Lord Kelvin (1824–1907), whose remarks spurred Marie to find the purest form of radium.

André Debierne became Marie's devoted lab partner after Pierre's death.

Röntgen's X-rays a hoax—Marie could not let it go unanswered. More than just the Curies' professional reputations were at stake; the new science of radioactivity, now in high-development mode, was in jeopardy.

From her point of view, nothing less than isolating the most pure form of radium—metallic radium—and establishing a more accurate atomic weight for it would do. She set about re-proving her discovery in such a way that no one could ever again doubt it. This effort, too, would take years. Now at her side was a faithful, longtime friend of the family and distinguished chemist, André Debierne.

In 1907, less than a year after Pierre's death, she determined the new atomic weight for radium, but it was not until 1910 that she isolated the metal in its purest form. At last, she wrote, "I saw the mysterious white metal."

The triumph was to be short-lived, however, for that year, 1910, would also mark the beginning of a period so difficult for Marie that it would nearly kill her.

A Loss Among Gains

Even while achieving that professional milestone, she was never far from the thought that she would soon suffer another grave loss. For nearly fifteen years, Dr. Eugène Curie had been much more than her father-in-law; he was a dear friend, valued confidant, beloved companion of Irène and Ève, and, simply, good company. In 1909, weakened by a severe case of pneumonia, he spent much of the year in bed, attended faithfully by Marie and Irène. On February 25, 1910, at eighty-two, he died. His absence from the lives of the Curie women was deeply felt. Thirteen-year-old Irène, in particular, suffered the loss of her closest friend and lifelong champion; six-year-old Ève lost the only father she had ever known. From now on, Marie would have to count on Polish governesses to help raise her daughters.

Although Marie's dedication to her work at this time helped to distract her from the family's personal loss, it also served to distract her from the worsening state of her own health. Friends and family again began to comment on how tired and worn she looked. Still, she continued her juggling act, teaching at the Sorbonne, carrying on her research at the lab, caring for her daughters, and becoming an increasingly active participant in the international scientific community.

She had, at least, stopped traveling to Sevres several times a week to teach classes there. Instead, she now had the added responsibility of planning for a new laboratory, which the university had agreed to fund. The project, which would take years to complete, would be called the Radium Institute.

In September, she traveled to Brussels, Belgium, to attend the World

This photo shows Dr. Eugène Curie, Pierre's father, in the garden at Sceaux. He lived with Marie and his granddaughters until his death in 1910.

Congress on Radiology and Electricity in order to help define an international radium standard. It had become necessary to "be able to control the relative purity of commercially produced radium," because the element was now in use all over the world, in medicine, industry, and research. The meeting was a difficult one, complete with displays of bad temper and bad manners. In the end, however, the men (Marie was the only woman in attendance) agreed to call the standard the *Curie*, based on Marie's definition of the measurement.

The project, which would take years to complete, would be called the Radium Institute.

She returned from Brussels, completed her book *A Treatise on Radioactivity*, and then late in the month went on vacation with her daughters and some family and friends to a town on the coast of Brittany.

Upon her return to Paris in the fall, she made a decision she would come to regret.

Smear Campaign

In November 1910, Marie Curie reluctantly agreed to offer herself as a candidate to the French Academy of Sciences to fill the seat that had become available for a physicist. She did this with great reluctance, for she had witnessed firsthand how difficult it was to become a member of this influential institution, even for a man if he was considered an outsider. Pierre had been rejected by the academy upon his first attempt to join and was not accepted until he had won the Nobel Prize and international acclaim. As a woman and a foreigner, Marie was the ultimate outsider. Still, she knew her membership would have advantages for her laboratory, so she announced her candidacy.

Doing so set off a media frenzy unlike anything she had experienced in the wake of the Nobel Prize. In the past, however, most press coverage had been positive, focusing on the Curies' work and accomplishments and, more recently, Marie's brave efforts to carry on alone. Now it seemed there was an organized, deliberate attempt underway to destroy her.

The conservative press attacked her on every front—her birthplace, her religion, her gender. Her achievements were dismissed and attributed entirely to Pierre. She was scoffed at and made fun of; it was even suggested that she had criminal tendencies. The cover of one tabloid, the *Excelsior*, featured pictures of her made to look like police mug shots; and so-called expert proof of her criminal nature was supposedly based on a handwriting analysis and an investigation of the shape of her skull.

The only other candidate for the seat, Edouard Branly, had earned his scientific credentials in the field of wireless telegraphy. He fit the membership mold and had the support of the powerful French Catholic community; he had even been honored for his work by the pope.

Marie was not without her supporters, however, and a number of prominent scientists and the liberal press did their best to counteract the damage being done to her reputation by the scandal sheets. On the day the

The tabloid press in Paris engaged in a smear campaign to prevent Marie Curie from becoming a member of the French Academy of Sciences. Here, photos of her are made to look like criminal mug shots.

vote was taken, January 23, 1911, a mob gathered to hear the results. When Branly won by only one vote, a second vote had to be taken. This time he won by the needed two. Marie would never try again to join the academy.

Following the defeat at the French Academy of Sciences, Marie, as usual, retreated into her work. Unfortunately, she could not retreat far enough to escape the long arm and prying eyes of the press. Even as she was preparing to go to Brussels to attend the Solvay Conference, a gathering of the world's top physicists, journalists from the French tabloids were gathering as well to launch a new attack on Marie, whose name in the headlines was guaranteed to sell papers.

Triumph Lost in Scandal

Ernest Solvay, a wealthy industrialist, had invited the twenty most accomplished scientists in the world to be his guests at a conference whose theme was radiation and quantum theory. Marie, of course, was the lone woman attending. Among the other "names" were Albert Einstein, who had revealed his famous equation, $E=mc^2$, in 1905; Ernest Rutherford, who discovered radon; and Henri Poincaré, the brilliant mathematician. Also in attendance was Paul Langevin, a former student of Pierre Curie and his successor at the School of Physics and Chemistry. Langevin also was a longtime member of the Curies' inner circle of friends and colleagues.

First Woman Admitted to the Academy of Sciences: Marguerite Perey

Marie Sklodowska-Curie may have failed to break through the all-male barrier at the French Academy of Sciences in 1911, but her presence could be felt when, nearly a half-century later, Marguerite Perey (1909–1975) became the first woman member of the academy in 1962. Perey began her scientific career in 1929 in Marie's laboratory, serving as her personal assistant. In 1939, at the age of twenty-nine, Perey, like her mentor, discovered a new chemical element. Francium (named for France) was given the number 87 on the Periodic Table, next to radium, number 88. The last element to be discovered in nature, francium today is used primarily in biological research and investigations into atomic structure.

Marguerite Perey (1909–1975), former assistant to Marie Curie, became the first woman member of the French Academy of Sciences in 1962.

Marie Curie was the only woman in attendance at the first Solvay Conference, held in Brussels, Belgium, in November 1911.

Feeling ill much of the time during the conference, Marie was forced to leave several meetings, but she stayed involved, meeting privately with Rutherford one night and writing a lengthy critique of the paper Einstein presented. Then, on November 4, 1911, her world came crashing down. Confronting her in the lobby of her hotel as she was leaving for the morning session of the conference were reporters, one of them shoving an issue of the French newspaper *Le Journal* in her face. It was then she learned she was being accused of having an affair with Paul Langevin, a married man with four children.

Though both Marie and Langevin denied the charges in writing, the story caught on like wildfire and had all the ingredients of the type of scandal the press feed upon and the public eat up—a troubled marriage, alleged love letters, murderous threats, even a duel. The sordid facts became irrelevant and Marie was painted as the villain of the story. Hunted by reporters and photographers, she was forced to take her daughters and seek shelter with friends to protect them and herself from harassment.

During the worst of the scandal, Marie received the news that she had been awarded a second Nobel Prize, this time for Chemistry. The press paid hardly any attention to this unprecedented achievement, choosing instead to fuel the flames of the sensational fire they had set weeks before. The members of the Swedish Academy of Sciences, fearing her appearance at the award ceremony would spoil the occasion, asked her not to attend. She replied, "In fact the prize was given to me for the discovery of radium and polonium. I think there is absolutely no connection between my scientific work and the facts of my private life, which uninformed and disreputable people use against me."

Shown is an undated photograph of Paul Langevin, taken many years after the scandal. He was a distinguished scientist and friend of the Curies.

Though quite seriously ill and very depressed, Marie was determined to back up her words, and so she made the forty-eight hour trip to Stockholm, accompanied by her sister Bronya and daughter Irène. The unpleasant disruption the Swedes feared her presence would cause never happened. Her lecture at the Nobel awards ceremony, given on December 11, 1911, began with a tribute to Pierre and ended with the sound of thunderous applause.

The Nobel Prize

Alfred Nobel (1833–1866), a Swedish scientist and inventor, at age thirty-three invented dynamite and the device used to ignite it, the blasting cap. By patenting his inventions, he became a multimillionaire. As he grew older, he became increasingly uncomfortable with the use of dynamite in warfare. As he neared the end of his life, he wanted to leave behind a very different legacy. With no family to inherit his great fortune, he left most of his estate to fund annual prizes in five areas of study—physics, chemistry, literature, peace, and medicine or physiology.

The first Nobel Prizes were awarded in 1901. Wilhelm Röntgen, the man who discovered X-rays, received the first Nobel in Physics. Only three people besides Marie Sklodowska-Curie have ever received two: Linus Pauling (for chemistry and peace), John Bardeen (both for physics), and Frederick Sanger (both for chemistry). An organization, the International Committee of the Red Cross, has won the most—three (all for peace). Of the total 797 Nobel Prize winners, only thirty-four have been women.

This is a painting of Alfred Nobel, inventor of dynamite, who later established the Nobel Prizes.

While she was in Stockholm, the papers reported that the Langevins had reached an amicable separation agreement; Marie's name was not mentioned.

In late December, Marie returned to Paris an international celebrity, even though some in her adopted country continued to hound the woman who had brought such glory to France. She was seriously ill now with a severe kidney infection and high fever. So weakened by the events of the preceding two years, she nearly died following the surgery she underwent to correct the damage to her kidneys (probably caused by overexposure to radium), and she would spend much of the next two years trying to regain her health—and her privacy.

By the summer of 1914, Marie had survived her war with the media and her battle against illness. No longer front-page news, she was able to return to work in her lab

Marie Curie is shown here in her office at the Radium Institute.

and in the classroom without being followed. In July, construction on the Radium Institute was at last complete, her office ready for its famous occupant.

Now, however, looming on the horizon was another war, a world war, one that would touch the lives of people everywhere.

CHAPTER 10

War Service

The dominant duty imposed on every one at that time was to help the country in whatever way possible during the extreme crisis that it faced.

In the early weeks of the summer of 1914, Marie had stayed in Paris, working. Her daughters, accompanied by a governess and a cook, had gone ahead without her to start their summer vacation in a little house on the seacoast of Brittany. By the end of July, Marie was looking forward to closing up the apartment she now lived in, locking the door on the laboratory, and joining them.

Then came the news all French citizens were dreading: The invading forces of Germany were on France's doorstep. On August 1, Marie wrote to Irène and Ève: "Things seem to be getting worse. . . . Don't be afraid; be calm and courageous." She assured them that if war did break out, she would send for them as soon as possible.

On the Battlefront

War did break out. The German army was marching across Belgium, and Poland was already partially controlled by enemy troops. What of her family

This notification called for the women of France to do whatever they could to support the war effort.

there? For now, Marie would have to live with not knowing. What she did know was that if she could not help her homeland, she had to do something to help her adopted country.

An odd sort of quiet had fallen over Paris: the quiet brought on by the absence of people. The government had moved to Bordeaux, a city in the southwest of France. All men capable of serving had left to join the regiments; thousands of others had fled to safety outside the city. The halls echoed with emptiness at the brand-new Radium Institute, where Marie remained alone with one technician, whose weak heart made him unfit for military service. What should she do? What *could* she do?

. . . if she could not help her homeland, she had to do something to help her adopted country.

The answer came quickly. When the French government realized the country's only supply of radium—now worth a million francs—might be dangerous if it fell into enemy hands, they ordered it moved from Paris. Marie herself would transport the precious cargo to Bordeaux for safekeeping. She boarded a packed train, with the heavy lead box containing the radium placed at her feet by a government official. Marie arrived in Bordeaux late in the day to find the city overrun and not a hotel room anywhere. Fortunately, a passing ministry employee found her lodgings for the night and carried her prized possession for her. Early the next day, with the box now entrusted to a bank vault, she doubled back to Paris aboard a military train.

She arrived home to some good news: For now, the German army had been turned back. She sent for her daughters and then began to search for some way to be of meaningful help during the conflict. Marie learned that most French hospitals throughout the country lacked X-ray equipment. This, she knew, would cost lives, the lives of wounded soldiers. With X-rays, doctors could pinpoint the location of bullets and shrapnel and more easily and safely remove them; without X-rays, they would be working blind.

Creating Mobile X-ray Stations

Marie Curie wasted no time in mobilizing. Her first stop was to gain permission from the minister of war to put into action a two-part plan she devised. The first part was to gather as much X-ray equipment as she could find. With it, in August and September 1914, she set up several radiology stations in the city.

The real need, however, was on the front, where the fighting was taking place and the men were falling. To meet this need, she had to implement part two of her plan: to create mobile radiology stations. Thus began her days of charming, persuading, and pleading with the wealthy to donate their automobiles to be refitted for service in the field. She also sought donations to buy everything needed to turn these vehicles into traveling X-ray units.

A photo of Marie shows her in her "little Curie" with no doors. In this clumsy-looking vehicle, she traveled all over France during World War I, taking X-rays of wounded soldiers and training others to use the equipment.

With help from the French Red Cross, by October 1914 twenty *petite Curies* (little Curies) were built. One of those vehicles she kept for herself, for she intended to be part of the action. She also recognized that her most important job was to train doctors, nurses, and volunteers on how to use the equipment. Expanding the scope of the radiology stations was essential in order to reach as many of the wounded as possible.

There were several problems, however, before she could implement this ambitious plan. First, though she had given lectures on X-rays, she had never worked with them, so she would have to teach herself how to use the equipment before she could train others. She also had to give herself a cram course in human anatomy. Second, she did not know how to drive, so at age fifty-three she would have to learn to do that as well—along with some basics about auto repair, such as how to change a tire and clean a dirty carburetor.

The most difficult aspect of this monumental effort, however, was not in getting the equipment or in training herself and others how to use it. It was in bypassing bureaucracy and overcoming

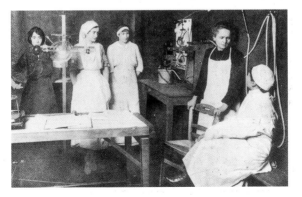

Marie Curie (second from right) is shown here with some of the nurses she trained as X-ray technicians during World War I.

resistance to change. The powers that be, including some of the field surgeons, did not want non-Army interference, especially from a woman—and a mere volunteer at that. Marie, with her usual determination, overcame all obstacles, one by one, eventually overseeing the start-up of two hundred stationary radiology stations and training more than one hundred fifty volunteer nurses to serve as technicians.

A Second Curie Partnership Begins

Her daughters were back in Paris now and in school, but they saw very little of their mother. If she was home for more than a day or two, Irène and Ève knew it meant she was ill—her kidney problems still forced her to take to her bed on occasion. Eventually, Irène, seventeen, insisted on being allowed to join the radiology service and, with Marie's permission, took a nursing course. Soon she was on the road with her mother, learning firsthand how to perform radiological examinations. By the time she turned eighteen, on September 12, 1915, she was competent enough to be left in charge of one of the radiology stations in Belgium.

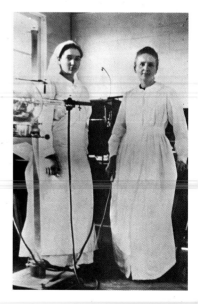

When the war ended on November 11, 1918, the victory for Marie was twice as sweet. For the first time in one hundred and fifty years, her beloved Poland was

Irène Curie (left), at seventeen, joined her mother and the war effort.

a free and independent state. "I had lived . . . to see the reparation of more than a century of injustice that had been done to Poland, my native country, and that had kept her in slavery," she wrote. After many years of separation, she was finally able to return to Warsaw, now capital of a free Poland, and see her family.

This image shows crowds cheering as the last German soldiers leave Poland. After more than a century, Marie's homeland was again an independent country.

Thanks to Marie's efforts during the four-year conflict, more than a million X-rays had been taken and countless lives had been saved. Yet when the war was over, the French government saw fit to award only Irène a military medal in recognition of her service to the country. Marie received nothing.

Building the Radium Institute

For another year, 1919–1920, Marie continued to do work related to the war. She offered courses in radiology to American soldiers who remained stationed in France, and she wrote a book, *Radiology in War*, detailing her experiences and all she had learned to advance the science of radiology and the understanding of X-ray technology.

Finally, in 1920, her eyesight failing now, she was able to begin work on the project closest to her heart: the development of the Radium Institute. To turn it into the world-class facility she imagined, she would need funding. That meant appealing to others for assistance and, more difficult for her, taking advantage of her international celebrity. So at fifty-five, Marie Curie went on the fund-raising road for her Radium Institute.

Among early contributors in France was the multimillionaire Henri de Rothschild, who gave Marie grants, which she used to pay her scientific staff. (One of those, Frédéric Joliot, would become Irène's husband and collaborator.) It was the Americans who came through for Marie most dramatically, however; and, ironically, it was thanks to a member of the dreaded press.

Marie "Missy" Meloney, an editor on the *Delineator*, an important women's magazine of the day, was an accomplished journalist who did not take no for an answer. She had been trying for years to get Marie to agree to an interview. Finally, the meeting took place. Though very different, the two women connected, and when

So at fifty-five, Marie Curie went on the fund-raising road for her Radium Institute.

Meloney learned Marie's laboratory had only a gram of radium and that America had fifty, she decided then and there to get Marie a second gram. She launched a "Marie Curie Radium Campaign," and within a year had raised $100,000, the current market price for a gram of the element. She also arranged to have Marie and her daughters go to the United States in 1921, where the president of the United States would present her with the radium at the White House.

The six-week visit was memorable for all the Curie women— though it was so exhausting for the ailing Marie that, from time to time, she had to send Irène or Ève to events in her place. From coast to coast, she was treated like royalty. She received honorary

Marie Curie is shown here on the arm of President Warren Harding on her first trip to the United States in 1921. He presented her with a gram of radium, paid for by the women of America.

degrees from universities throughout the country, met with great American scientists, and saw many of the great sights, including Niagara Falls and the Grand Canyon.

When she returned to France on June 25, 1921, it was with much more than just the gram of radium; the generous Americans had also given her valuable ore samples, equipment, and a number of cash awards from scientific organizations. She would spend the rest of her life "building up for those who will come after me an Institute of Radium such as I wish, to the memory of Pierre Curie and to the highest interest of humanity."

CHAPTER 11

The Last Years

We must believe that we are gifted for something, and that thing at whatever cost, must be attained.

Though small, fragile-looking, and soft-spoken, *la patronne* ("the boss") inevitably intimidated researchers and lab workers who came to interview for positions at her laboratory. Her uniform black dress and cold expression did not help put them at ease. It was only upon talking to her about scientific research that her face relaxed, her **cataract**-clouded eyes showed a glimpse of their former light, and an extraordinary smile spread across her face.

If they gained the right to work with the "living library of radium," they would experience daily this woman's interest in the smallest detail of every procedure and every discovery that took place in her laboratory. She could be

infuriating, there was no doubt—no one could be more stubborn and demanding. But to those who proved their worth, along with their desire to work hard and learn, no one could be kinder or more caring. These researchers were her extended family, living together in a house of science.

This photo shows Marie Curie with the look on her face that intimidated newcomers to her lab at the Radium Institute.

Irène Curie (1897–1956)

In 1926 at age twenty-nine, Irène Curie married Frédéric Joliot, who began work as a junior lab assistant at the Radium Institute. In 1935, the couple would win the Nobel Prize in Chemistry for their discovery of **artificial radioactivity**. For thirty-two years, Marie was the only woman to receive a Nobel Prize. Her daughter Irène became the second.

Irène Curie is photographed here with the man who would become her husband, Frédéric Joliot.

Irène died at age fifty-eight on March 17, 1956, of leukemia, believed to have been caused by her war work with X-rays and lifelong exposure to radioactive substances.

One of those researchers was a member of her actual family. Irène, like her mother, had earned her PhD in physics, in March 1925, from the Sorbonne. Her thesis was titled "On the **Alpha Rays** of Polonium," a study of the first element her mother had discovered. A crowd gathered on this occasion as it had more than twenty years earlier. If they had come to see Marie, they were disappointed. She had stayed home, so as not to draw attention away from her daughter.

Ève Curie (1904–2007)

Ève Curie, the only nonscientist in the family, was trained as a concert pianist, but she found her real calling in writing. She became famous for the best-selling biography she wrote of her mother, *Madame Curie*, in 1937, which was turned into a movie in 1943.

Though lacking the science gene, Ève did share the family trait of patriotism, serving with the Fighting French during the Nazi occupation of her country in World War II. She also wrote a book called *Journey Among Warriors*, detailing her forty-thousand-mile trip across wartime fronts.

Although she was the only member of her family not to win a Nobel Prize, she married a man who did. Henry Richardson Labouisse, the director of UNICEF, accepted the Nobel Peace Prize on behalf of that organization in 1965.

Ève Curie died in New York City on October 22, 2007, at the age of one hundred and two. She is said to have felt guilty all her life that she alone had not suffered the consequences of radiation poisoning.

Ève Curie, the only nonscientist in the family, became an accomplished pianist and author.

From Miserable Shed to Multimillion-Dollar Institute

As soon as she had recovered from her trip to the United States in 1921 and until her death, Marie Curie's life centered on equipping and enhancing the laboratory housed in one of the twin brick and stone buildings on Rue des Nourices (now Rue Pierre Curie). In contrast, she left virtually empty the large, beautiful apartment she had moved into following her kidney operation, and where she would live for the last twenty-two years of her life with her daughter Ève. Only her study there was furnished comfortably, her books and papers presided over by a portrait of Pierre.

Originally, the Radium Institute was composed of two laboratory facilities, one dedicated to the study of the physics and chemistry of radioactivity, headed by Marie, and the other dedicated to the study of its medical applications. Over time, and thanks in large part to the tireless nurturing of its famous director, the institute would grow into an enormous complex and the number of researchers from a few to dozens. And though it exhausted her and kept her

Marie Curie, on her second trip to the United States, is photographed here in 1929.

from her own research, she traveled increasingly now (including another trip to America in 1929), in a never-ending quest to add to the institute's store of radioactive sources so that she and her staff could continue to unravel the mystery of radioactive elements.

Unraveling the Effects of Radium

Throughout the 1920s, the Radium Institute continued to grow in size, wealth, and reputation. Growing at the same time, however, were reports of incidents of illness and death—including a number of Marie's colleagues and coworkers—that seemed directly related to contact with the radiation emitted by radium and other radioactive substances. How could it be that this element, which had shown such promise as a cure for disease, now be accused of *causing* injury, disease, and even death?

> . . . it was discovered that radium, or the radiation it gives off, can both kill and cure.

As the science of radiation developed, it was discovered that radium, or the radiation it gives off, can both kill and cure. Radium behaves chemically like calcium, and tends to migrate to the bones, where most calcium is found; there the radiation it gives off begins to kill the cells that produce red blood cells, and can cause cancer in the **bone marrow**.

It is now known that radium emits several different kinds of radiation. Some are highly dangerous, others are not; and some of the most dangerous can be harnessed for the good of humanity. The risk level also depends on the amount and length of exposure. **Gamma rays**, such as those given off in a nuclear explosion, are the most dangerous, because they cannot be stopped by human skin and so can damage cells anywhere in the body and cause cancer. Gamma radiation can also be used to kill cancer cells. Alpha rays, in contrast, cannot travel very deeply

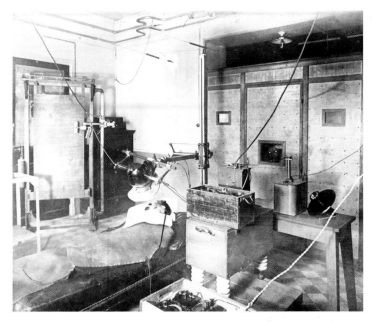

Early cancer treatment used a combination of radium and X-rays. Only the part of the patient's body to be treated is exposed; the rest is covered with lead-rubber, a material that cannot be pierced by radium rays. The equipment operator stands behind a lead-glass window at the rear of the room.

into human skin and so are dangerous only if their source is embedded in the body. **Beta particles** are in between these two types of radiation—they can penetrate short distances into the body.

There are many reasons scientists had trouble unraveling the mystery of radiation's "multiple personality": Depending on how much and how long the exposure, it typically takes a long time for the effects of radiation poisoning, or radiation illness, to show up. Also, exposure to radiation affects different people differently. As with smoking, some people become sick very early, while others can smoke their entire lives and live to

The Radium Girls

Probably the most well-known case of radiation poisoning resulted from the use of a brand of paint called Undark, which contained radium to make it glow in the dark. Produced in the years from 1917 to 1926 by the U.S. Radium Corporation based in central New Jersey, Undark was used primarily to paint the numbers and hands on watch and clock faces, as well as the dials on the instrument panels in aircraft. (The U.S. military was a major customer.) Young girls and women were hired to do this delicate handwork, and they were instructed to "point" the tips of the brushes with their lips and tongues. Over time, many of the girls began to suffer from cancer, bone decay, anemia, tooth loss, and infections of the jaw.

"Radium girls" working in a factory at the U.S. Radium Corporation did not know they were being exposed to danger.

In 1927, five dial painters filed a lawsuit against U.S. Radium, asking $250,000 each in compensation. A year later they were each awarded $10,000, plus $600 a year and payment for medical expenses for as long as each suffered from radium poisoning and its effects—essentially the rest of their lives. They did not live long: all died from radiation-induced cancer within a few years. To this day, some of their graves are still radioactive.

a ripe, old age. The most immediate reason scientists did not focus on the danger was that, in the right hands, particularly in the hands of doctors, radiation had been proven effective in treating cancer.

For years, Marie had known that working closely with radiation posed risks, but like other scientists of the time was unclear exactly what the health effects of exposure were. How much was too much? As a precaution in the lab at the Radium Institute, radioactive sources were enclosed in lead, and protective screens were installed to separate workers from the source. She also required her staff to have their blood counts checked regularly.

Still, she was reluctant to admit what the mounting evidence was telling her. Was she not proof? Had she not spent years isolating radium under the worst possible conditions, and with no protection at all? At the same time, her suspicions were growing. As early as 1920, nearly blinded by cataracts and tormented by continuous humming in her ears, she wrote to Bronya, "Perhaps radium has something to do with these troubles, but it cannot be affirmed with certainty. . . . Don't speak of them to anybody, above all things."

Working Until the End

Marie continued to work, using various methods to disguise her "troubles" from her coworkers until she underwent four cataract surgeries, the last in 1930. Her sight partially restored, she began to struggle more with a loss of courage, questioning whether she should quit working, move to the country, and take up gardening. Still, she could not waver from her mission; and as her health deteriorated, she worried more, especially about the future of the Radium Institute.

This 1938 photograph shows the Radium Institute in Paris, France.

In late 1933, she suffered a gall bladder attack and refused an operation in favor of more exercise. By Easter 1934, she was organizing a trip to the south of France with Bronya, where Marie caught the flu. Even in bed she worked on what would be her last book, *Radioactivity*.

When Missy Meloney had asked Marie years earlier to write her autobiography, she had replied, "It will not be much of a book. It is such an uneventful, simple little story." The simple little story came to an end on July 4, 1934. At the age of sixty-six, Marie Sklodowska-Curie died in a sanatorium in the French Alps. Her daughter, Ève, was by her side.

CHAPTER 12

Marie Curie's Legacy

She did not know how to be famous.

—*Ève Curie*

Marie Sklodowska-Curie may not have known how to be famous, but famous she became. Even today she is one of a very small number of women scientists widely known by name.

How this woman triumphed over political tyranny, poverty, gender bias, personal tragedy, and scandal and changed not just the course of science but also the course of the world is truly a remarkable human story. Yet she never found it so. She once summed up her life in twenty-five words: "I was born in Warsaw of a family of teachers. I married Pierre Curie and had two children. I have done my work in France."

Since then, others have found much more to say about the life of Marie Curie. It would be difficult, in fact, to calculate the number of words written about her or to measure her enormous influence.

Name Recognition

If she had done nothing more than inspire generations of young people, Marie Curie's life would be counted a phenomenal success. Her influence remains powerful today, nearly seventy years after her death. She has even become something of a pop culture figure, her image gracing T-shirts and posters—one reading, "When I Grow Up, I

Want to Be a Marie Curie." Her likeness has appeared on the currency (both coins and bills) of countries all over the world; postage stamps, too. There is even an asteroid named after her. And as recently as 2007, a métro stop in Paris was renamed the Pierre and Marie Curie station.

This postage stamp from Senegal, in West Africa, honors the Curies and the discovery of radium in 1898.

It's questionable whether she would appreciate those kinds of tributes; but lover of learning that she was, she might be pleased to know of the numerous educational institutions around the globe that bear her (and sometimes Pierre's) name. Hotels, clinics, streets, museums, and hospitals likewise are named for her. In the world of science, the *Curie* is the term for a unit of radioactivity; curium is the 96th element in the Periodic Table; and curite, sklodowskite, and cuprosklodowskite are three radioactive minerals.

And what of her scientific legacy, beyond the now-famous name? In Marie Curie's last years, her elements, polonium and radium, which she often regarded as her "children," had become more like problem children. Their reputations, like that of their "celebrity mom," have seesawed since their discovery in 1898, from miraculous cure to menacing killer.

In that time, scientists and researchers have discovered a

This sign in Paris indicates the street named for the Curies.

great deal more about them—in particular the radiation they give off. The Curies opened the field of radioactive science, which led off into many other directions, most notably atomic energy and the nuclear industry, both with the potential to do enormous good or horrendous evil. In recent decades, it is the evil and harmful uses of radioactivity that have taken center stage, directing all attention away from the thousands of ways it can and does benefit humanity every day.

Whether in the future radiation is used to heal or to harm, to build or destroy, is in human hands.

Marie's Final First

The day after Marie died, the headline in the *New York Times* called her a "martyr to science." Was she a martyr? Had she sacrificed everything to her work? Or was she just a woman who found the work she loved to do and dedicated her life to doing it? She and Pierre had worked hard, yes, and they had suffered at times, financially and personally. But they had lived the scientific dream Pierre had imagined when he wrote to Marie forty years earlier, hoping to convince her to "pass our lives near each other."

The day after Marie died, the headline in the New York Times *called her a "martyr to science."*

Two days after she died, on July 6, 1934, Marie Curie was laid to rest according to her wishes, with only family and close friends and colleagues in attendance. Her plain oak coffin was placed on top of Pierre's at the cemetery in Sceaux, the village where their two lives became joined. In full bloom was the climbing rosebush she had planted at the gravesite after Pierre's death. Her sister Bronya and brother Jòzef buried with her what mattered most to their youngest sister: handfuls of earth from her beloved Poland.

Radiation Today

In medicine, radiation is used to diagnose and treat illnesses. Every year, according to one estimate, seven out of ten Americans are given radiation therapy of one form or another, and are diagnosed using X-rays, CAT scans, or MRIs. Radiation is used in the food industry to kill bacteria and preserve food without chemicals or refrigeration. Contact lens solutions are treated with radiation to ensure they are pure enough to put in human eyes.

Radiation techniques are used by forensic scientists to solve crimes by enabling them, for example, to trace the path of a gunshot or of a suspect's footsteps or to find fingerprints. In agriculture, radiation is used to control insects, avoiding the use of dangerous pesticides. In the kitchen, microwave ovens are standard features, as is nonstick cookware, which is treated with gamma rays.

The smoke detectors and alarms required in homes today contain small amounts of radioactive material, as do the runway lights at many airports. Radiation is used in archaeology, to carbon-date ancient artifacts and sites. In short, there is almost no industry, field of study, or aspect of human life in which radiation technology does not play some role.

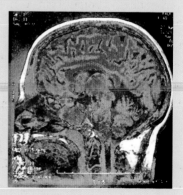

Today, radiation is widely used in medicine for diagnostic purposes, as in this MRI of the human brain.

In a grand ceremony on April 20, 1995, the Curies' coffins were moved to the Pantheon in Paris.

For more than sixty years, there the Curies rested. Then, on April 20, 1995, the coffins of the two publicity-shy scientists were moved from the serenity of the Parisian countryside to the Pantheon, France's most celebrated mausoleum for its great men. Now, for the first time, it would contain a great woman honored for her own accomplishments. (In 1907, Sophie Berthelot was allowed to be buried at the Pantheon alongside her husband, chemist and politician Marcellin Berthelot.)

The ceremony was in stark contrast to the Curies' original burials. This one was attended by thousands, who lined the white-carpeted street leading up to the steps of the Pantheon to watch the two coffins being carried by soldiers of the French Republic Guard. French President François Mitterand dedicated his speech to the women of France as he praised Marie Curie's "remarkable battle." He then quoted something Marie had said just a year before her death: "I am among those who think that science has great beauty. I do not believe that in our world the spirit of adventure is at risk of disappearing."

How fitting that her words should be repeated just steps away from the site of the miserable old shed where Marie Curie's own adventure had begun.

Glossary

alpha rays—streams of positively charged particles emitted by certain radioactive materials. An alpha particle is one of the three types of radiation resulting from natural radioactivity. *See also:* beta particles, gamma rays, and radioactivity.

artificial radioactivity—a non-radioactive element that has been made radioactive by bombarding it with atomic particles.

atomic weight—the total mass of protons and neutrons in the nucleus (the positively charged center) of a single atom.

barometer—a device used to measure atmospheric pressure, the pressure exerted by Earth's atmosphere.

beta particles—electrons emitted during radioactive decay and one of the three types of radiation resulting from natural radioactivity. *See also:* alpha rays, gamma rays, and radioactivity.

bone marrow—soft tissue that fills the cavities of most animal bones, including those of humans.

cataract—an abnormality of the eye marked by clouding of the lens, which prevents light from passing through and thus impeding sight.

crystal—in chemistry, a solid body of an element whose structure is marked by a regular, repeating pattern of its atoms and, often, its external plane surfaces that form distinctive angles.

electroscope—an instrument used to detect an electric charge of a body, or to determine whether a charge is positive or negative; also used to measure levels of radiation.

fluorescent—having light emitting from an object, produced by bombardment of other kinds of electromagnetic radiation, such as X-rays or ultraviolet rays.

fractional crystallization—a process used to separate a chemical compound into its components.

gamma rays—one of the three types of radiation resulting from natural radioactivity. A gamma ray is a photon emitted spontaneously by a radioactive substance. *See also:* alpha rays, beta particles, and radioactivity.

inert—in chemistry, lacking in active properties; absence of expected reaction.

magnetism—the attractive or repulsive force exerted on materials by the motion of charged particles.

ores—minerals or rocks that contain metal and that can be mined at a profit.

radioactivity—emission of radiation, energy transmitted as particle rays or waves. *See also:* alpha rays, beta particles, and gamma rays.

rubles—Russian currency (money) in use in Poland while ruled by the Russian Empire.

rue—the French word for *street*.

sanatorium—a health facility for treating the chronically ill.

Bibliography

Books

Brian, Denis. *The Curies: A Biography of the Most Controversial Family in Science*. Hoboken, NJ: John Wiley & Sons, Inc., 2005.

Clark, Claudia. *Radium Girls: Women and Industrial Health Reform, 1910–1935*. Chapel Hill, NC: University of North Carolina Press, 1997.

Curie, Ève. *Madame Curie: A Biography*. Translated by Vincent Sheean. Garden City, NY: Doubleday, Doran & Company, Inc., 1937.

Curie, Marie. *Pierre Curie, with Autobiographical Notes* (Introduction by Mrs. William Brown Meloney). New York: Macmillan, 1923.

Giroud, Fancoise. *Marie Curie: A Life*. Translated by Lydia Davis. New York: Holmes and Meier Publishers, Inc., 1986.

Goldsmith, Barbara. *Obsessive Genius: The Inner World of Marie Curie*. New York: W. W. Norton & Company, 2005.

Isaacson, Walter. *Einstein: His Life and Universe*. New York: Simon & Schuster, 2007.

Pasachoff, Naomi. *Marie Curie and the Science of Radioactivity*. New York and Oxford, UK: Oxford University Press, 1996.

Pflaum, Rosalynd. *Grand Obsession: Madame Curie and Her World*. New York: Doubleday, 1989.

Quinn, Susan. *Marie Curie: A Life*. New York: Simon & Schuster, 1995.

Reid, Robert William. *Marie Curie*. New York: Saturday Review Press, 1974.

Steele, Philip. *Marie Curie: The Woman Who Changed the Course of Science*. Washington, DC: National Geographic Children's Books, 2006.

Waltar, Alan E. *Radiation and Modern Life. Fulfilling Marie Curie's Dream*. Amherst, NY: Prometheus Books, 2004.

Articles

Grady, Denise. "A Glow in the Dark, and a Lesson in Scientific Peril." *New York Times*, October 6, 1998, p. F4.

Mould, R. F. "The Discovery of Radium in 1898 by Maria Sklodowska-Curie and Pierre Curie, with Commentary on Their Life and Times." *The British Journal of Radiology*, 71 (1998): pp. 1229–1254.

Sklodowska-Curie, Marie. "Radium and Radioactivity." *Century Magazine*, January 1904, pp. 461–466.

Web Sites

Curie, Pierre. Nobel lecture, The Nobel Prize in Physics, 1903. www.nobelprize.org.

Froman, Nancy. "Marie and Pierre Curie and the Discovery of Polonium and Radium," December 1, 1996. www.nobelprize.org.

"In Praise of Pierre and Marie Curie," excerpts of François Mitterand's speech at the interment of the Curies at the Pantheon; translated by William Evenson. *History of Physics Newsletter*, American Physical Society. vol. vi, no. v, October 1996; http://units.aps.org (accessed February 2008).

"It's Elemental: The Element Radium," Jefferson Lab. http://education.jlab.org/itselemental/ele088.html (accessed August 3, 2007).

"Marie Curie and the Science of Radioactivity," American Institute of Physics (AIP). www.aip.org/history/curie (accessed June 2008).

Maria Sklodowska-Curie Museum Web site run by the Polish Chemical Society. www.ptchem.lodz.pl/en/museum.html (accessed January 2008).

"Radiation Information," U.S. Environmental Protection Agency. www.epa.gov (accessed July 15, 2007).

Source Notes

The following list identifies the sources of the quoted material found in this book. The first and last few words of each quotation are cited, followed by the source. Complete information on each source can be found in the Bibliography.

Abbreviations:
TC—*The Curies*
MCB—*Madame Curie: A Biography*
PC—*Pierre Curie, with Autobiographical Notes*
NL—*Nobel lecture by Pierre Curie*
MPCDPR—"Marie and Pierre Curie and the Discovery of Polonium and Radium": Nobelprize.org Web site
HPN—*History of Physics Newsletter*: American Physical Society Web site
RML—*Radiation and Modern Life*

INTRODUCTION: A Glow in the Dark
PAGE 1 *"The glowing tubes . . . faint, fairy lights."*: PC, p. 187

CHAPTER 1: Youngest and Brightest
PAGE 2 *"I was only . . . forward to recite."*: PC, p. 158
PAGE 5 *"physics apparatus."*: MCB, p. 16
PAGE 10 *"This catastrophe . . . profound depression."*: PC, p. 157
PAGE 12 *"Ah, how gay . . . hardly imagine."*: MCB, p. 40

CHAPTER 2: An Independent Life
PAGE 14 *"Thus, when . . . an independent life."*: PC, p. 163
PAGES 14–15 *"That going . . . those I loved."*: PC, p. 163
PAGE 15 *"excellent people."*: MCB, p. 16
PAGE 18 *"I was as . . . and physics."*: PC, p. 165
PAGE 18 *"acquired the habit . . . later on."*: PC, p. 166
PAGE 18 *"the marvelous . . . snow plains."*: PC, p. 164
PAGE 20 *"If they don't . . . to the devil!"*: MCB, p. 77
PAGE 21 *"I dreamed of . . . what to do."*: MCB, p. 84
PAGE 22 *"At times I . . . physics and chemistry."*: PC, p. 167
PAGE 22 *"If you can't . . . it to you."*: MCB, p. 88

CHAPTER 3: Paris, and Pierre
PAGE 23 *"[A]t the age . . . for several years."*: PC, p. 169
PAGE 25 *"My situation . . . whom I knew."*: PC, p. 170
PAGE 29 *"tall young . . . limpid eyes,"*: PC, p. 173
PAGE 32 *"an existence . . . science,"*: PC, p. 173
PAGE 32 *"We have . . . scientific dream."*: MCB, p. 130
PAGE 33 *"It is a sorrow . . . separating."*: MCB, p. 136

CHAPTER 4: Match Made in Science
PAGE 34 *"My husband . . . time together."*: PC, p. 175
PAGE 38 *"I thus . . . quarters."*: PC, p. 178
PAGE 39 *"For more than . . . of spirits."*: TC, p. 49
PAGE 39 *"reach its end . . . go through."*: TC, p. 49
PAGE 40 *"soul flew away"*: MCB, p. 148
PAGE 40 *"I expect . . . you coming."*: TC, p. 49
PAGE 40 *"It became . . . scientific work."*: PC, p. 179
PAGE 41 *"It was under . . . years."*: PC, p. 180

CHAPTER 12: Marie Curie's Legacy
  PAGE 113 *"She did not . . . famous."*: MCB, p. x
  PAGE 113 *"I was born . . . in France."*: PC
  PAGE 115 *"pass our . . . each other."*: MCB, p. 130
  PAGE 117 *"remarkable battle."*: HPN, p. x.
  PAGE 117 *"I am among . . . disappearing."*: HPN, p. x

Image Credits

ACJC-Curie and Joliot-Curie Fund: 11, 19, 31, 56, 62, 63
© The Print Collector/Alamy: 3, 95
© Bettmann/Corbis: 17, 21, 51, 80, 101, 104, 107, 109
© DK Limited/Corbis: 5
© Hulton-Deutsch Collection/Corbis: 81, 90, 106
© Corbis/Sygma: 43
© Orban Thierry/Corbis Sygma: 117
© Underwood & Underwood/Corbis: 39
Emilio Segre Visual Archives: 33, 46, 48, 58, 91, 92, 93, 105
Claudecf/www.flickr.com: 28
Iris Christiani/bionerd/www.flickr.com: 55
Julie Falk/CaptPiper/www.flickr.com: 116
Kaustav Bhattacharya/www.flickr.com: 70
Richard Beck/becklectic/www.flickr.com: 114 (bottom)
Uncle Buddha/www.flickr.com: 24
Albert Harlingue/Roger Violett/Getty Images: 87
Hulton Archive/Getty Images: 23, 37, 60
John Phillips/Time Life Pictures/Getty Images: 112
Popperfoto/Getty Images: 13, 41, 68, 77, 100
Library of Congress: 6, 7, 25, 35, 36, 42, 44, 45, 53, 61, 73, 85, 94, 96, 103
Map by Jim McMahon: 8
Mary Evans Picture Library: 72, 82, 99
Musee Curie/ACJC/Institut Curie: 71, 75, 84
KPA/Newscom: 2, 10, 16, 50, 98
The Art Archive/Culver Pictures/The Picture Desk: 30
The Art Archive/Historical Museum Warsaw/Alfredo Dagli Orti/The Picture Desk: 4
www.med.yale.edu: 66
Cover art: © Bettmann/Corbis

About the Author

Janice Borzendowski is a Manhattan-based writer whose previous books include *John Russwurm*, a biography in the series Black Americans of Achievement, and *Caring for Your Aging Dog* and *Caring for Your Aging Cat*, comprehensive guides for senior pet care. Janice is also an experienced editor and ghost writer, in fields as wide-ranging as technology, sports, architecture, history, and science. Like Marie Sklodowska-Curie, Janice is proud of her Polish heritage and credits Madame Curie as her earliest role model.

Index